TOTAL MADNESS

by
George Marshall

S.T. Publishing

To my wife Rhona for all her love and support, and my son Scott for all his smiles and distractions.

Total Madness (pbk)

© George Marshall. 1993.

ISBN No. 0 9518497 4 3

Published by S.T. Publishing, Scotland.
Printed by Pyramid Press, England.
Typeset by Work, Rest And Play, Scotland.

Also by the same author:

The Two Tone Story (1990)
Spirit Of '69 - A Skinhead Bible (1991)
Bad Manners (1993)

A lot of music books are written by hacks with no real love of the band, a three week deadline and an overdose of photos. The idea is that if the publisher gets it out while interest is at its greatest, then the fans will buy anything. That's not what *Total Madness* is about. I'm no clever dick with words and will never be a great writer, but what I can offer is a fan's true love for one of the greatest bands I had the good fortune to bump into during my dance crazed youth. Mere pages don't even begin to capture the excitement and atmosphere generated by going to gigs, and record reviews are never a patch on what comes booming out of speakers, but hopefully this book will add something to the wonderful world of Madness for die-hard followers and casual fans alike. Special thanks to a certain Chris Foreman for his help with this book. They say you should never meet your heroes because they just shatter your illusions. Well, Mr. Foreman is definitely the exception to that rule.

Thanks too for the support and inspiration I receive from Udo Vogt, Mike Johnson, Richard Davenport, Lol Pryor, Mark Brennan, David Quinn, Jimmy and Jigs at the Merc, the mighty Gillingham F.C., Matzge at Pork Pie, Simon Playford, Bubbles at Sherry's, David Belcher, Stuart and Mark at Scootering, Arthur Kay, Ossi at Moskito, Jackie at Go Ahead, Dermott at Caroline, Thomas of SOS Bote, Fred Dornier and all the readers of *Skinhead Times*.

Ask a silly question . . .

Stiff/Nigel Illegible

"Can you imagine us at 30 leaping around on stage?"
Suggs, 1980.

Introducing From Right To Left . . .
Daniel "Woody" Woodgate, Chris "Chrissy Boy" Foreman, Graham "Suggs" McPherson, Mike "Barso" Barson, Carl "Chas Smash" Smyth, Mark "Bedders" Bedford and Lee "Kix" Thompson.

Teldec

Copies of this book were available to the readers of Skinhead Times in advance of publication. The first 100 buyers of Total Madness were

Brian Adelgaard, Harry Van Vliet, Mike Johnson, Oliver Söhn, Taru Pylkkonen, Kathy Sennott, Gary Annan, Nick Arnison, Katherine Weaver, Tony Baker, Mark Nichols, Dite Burns, Nick Hewitson, Debbie Houghton, C. Webster, Gail McGee, Wayne Dymond, Keith Wilkinson, Pete Horsley, Nicola Taylor, Puddy Waterhouse, P.R. Elvy, Phil Webb, Gavin Bates, Tom Thorn, Simon James, Ian Baillie, Iain Branks, Helly Woods, Katherine Woods and Tricky Dicky Woods, Lee Burchett, Chris Davidson, Alan Sinclair, Tony Price, Anthony Atkins, Wayne Frankland, C. Elrick, Alan Smith, Sean O'Toole, Steve and Michelle Fridd, Steve and Lynda Bedford, Jon Verrill, Chris Potter, Nicholas Cole, Steve Harrington, Graeme Proudfoot, Deb Fairclough, Phil Putman, Michael Cowan, Mark Rogers, Steve Hoare, Debi Laishley, Michael Collins, Dave Whittington, Dave Drew, Keith Leech, Alfonso Sacristan, Paul Oakman, Dominique Ruimy, Franck Etchegaray, Robert-Jan Breeman, Frank Wilmink, Don Goepfert, Clive Lennox, Michael Sinclair, John Rankin, Marcey Hall, Thomas Carnewal, Pieter Neefs, Serge Schryvers, Andreas Ihm, Einar Vadstein, Matt Bilby, G.P. Williams, Chris Wallis, Dave Inglis, Peter Levo, Jordi Ramirez, Toni Clarimunt, Javier Perez Madariaga, Brian Garvin, Jan Lund, Florian Ennoeckl, Francois La Grange, Thierry Greiner, Harry Mulder, Nick O'Brien, Edward Van Helden, Niklas C.V. Van Tran, Christian Dziallas, Stefan Menzner, Dirk Bocksrocker, Michael Gerth, Kai Budewig, Jörg Philipp, Beate Gläser, Thomas Christmann, Allison Holmes and Michael Gasperl.

TOTAL MADNESS
Contents

ALL IN THE MIND

When it comes to towns, cities and countries, absence really does make the heart grow fonder. Romanticism replaces realism as your mind's eye turns litter-filled back streets into green and pleasant lands. And the longer you're away, the bigger the fairy tale. Maybe that's why the biggest patriots tend to be those living in exile, forced or otherwise.

To one Graham McPherson, paradise lost was London. Not that he was born within the sound of Bow Bells or anything, but when you spend your childhood being passed from pillar to post, the bright lights of the Big Smoke can appear very attractive indeed. He was actually from the Sussex seaside town of Hastings, but didn't stay there very long.

His father walked out on the family when Graham was three, leaving his mum, a jazz singer, to bring his sister and him up. Single parents don't have it easy at the best of times, but when you're trying to make a living touring the pubs and clubs, family life ends up taking a back seat. The young Graham McPherson found himself living in far-flung cities of the old Empire, like Manchester and Liverpool, before being sent to live with his aunt in North Wales at the age of eight. At least one good thing came out of his connection with the music world though. His nickname, Suggs, was borrowed (and never returned) from a flautist in a jazz encyclopedia.

He spent four years in Wales, living the life of a yokel while dreaming of London and all it would offer him. More than anything, Suggs wanted to be part of the mod and skinhead gangs he read about in the 'papers. And come the day when his mum did decide to move back down south and settle in North London, Suggs was on his way to the big time. Well, that was the game plan anyway. The problem was that nobody had told the London kids what the game was.

When he arrived at Quinton Kynaston all boys' school in Swiss Cottage, not only was he treated like a country bumpkin, but the mod and skin gangs he had hoped to join were now a thing of the past. He still didn't belong and his childhood remained largely a solitary one. The moving from town to town hadn't helped academically, and his mum never made him go to school anyway, but he did get two O-levels and a CSE, and stayed on for the sixth form. It wasn't that he really wanted to, but it was worth his while to do so thanks to the social security rules of the day.

Gangs hadn't disappeared entirely however. One in particular, the Aldenham Glamour Boys, had a name for themselves in this neck of the woods. They were a peculiar mixture of suedeheads, teds and Roxy Music freaks who took their name from the Aldenham Boys Club that they frequented. Each was an outcast in his own way, but together they were something people took notice of, something to be reckoned with. Like all mobs, they got into fights with rival gangs, but such is growing up in the darker corners of any city you care to mention. *A Clockwork Orange* was showing in cinemas at the time and the Glamour Boys saw it countless times.

Stiff

Mind you, the same was true of that other film that threatened the
very fabric of society, *Dumbo*, which they were also regulars at.

Suggs first met the gang in a street in Hampstead and spent
the rest of the day knocking back pints with them. In a world of daft
flares and even dafter Kevin Keegan haircuts, the Aldenham
Glamour Boys stood out a mile. Spray-painted DMs and imported
Levi's 501 jeans were the order of the day, as were ex-G.P.O.
Morris Minor vans. Nothing but the best for these lads.

This was the life Suggs had been looking for, but little did he
know what fate had in store for him and certain Glamour Boys.
Among this motley crew of misfits were three blokes who had known
each other since primary school, and who Suggs was going to get to
know very well too. Step forward Chris Foreman, Mike Barson and
Lee Thompson.

Chrissy Boy Foreman had left Owen's Grammar School in
Islington with a single O-level to his name, and ended up doing a
series of dead-end jobs like hospital porter, and painter and
decorator. He and Lee actually worked together for a while as
gardeners for Camden Council which was a better laugh, but not
exactly a passport to the good life.

Lee came from the wrong side of the tracks and for a time
looked like he would stay there. He was brought up in a block of
flats on Highgate Road mainly by his mum, as his dad spent much
of his time behind bars. Young Thommo, as his mates called him,

was no angel either and soon rang up 13 court appearances himself. On his 14th birthday, he bunked off school and stole a bag from a hospital locker. In it was £130, mostly in coins, and he made the mistake of giving out handfuls of 50p pieces to his mates. Someone grassed on him, and Thommo ended up getting a kicking off the Old Bill and getting sent down from November 1971 to January '73. Chafford Approved School played host to him, but at least he was allowed out at weekends.

For his sins, Mike Barson had made it to Hornsey Art College, but dropped out after a year to pursue a career in spraying huge graffiti style pictures on walls. He was inspired by the New York subway gangs who had been featured in the Sunday supplements, and he didn't see any reason to confine himself to an artist's pad when virtually every brick in North London was crying out for a splash of paint. Lee was in on it too under the name of Kix, as was Chris on occasion, and one of their masterpieces of a car crash was later featured in a book by George Melley.

Mike's year at art school wasn't entirely wasted though because it was there that he began to teach himself the piano. In fact music was beginning to play a big part in all of their lives. Everyone in the gang listened to the same sort of stuff - Motown, The Coasters, Fats Domino, that sort of thing. Roxy Music were another big favourite as were local heroes Kilburn & The High Roads, Alex Harvey, and the seemingly immortal Gary Glitter, and they spent much of their time bunking into gigs.

By 1976, punk had arrived and was kicking a few backsides in the music business. Venues were starting to open their doors to inexperienced musicians and anybody who was anybody was in a band. With that knowledge and a bit of guidance from his brother Ben, Mike decided to form a group. Chris and Lee had always said they'd start a band, so were natural candidates to join. The fact that neither could play a note was a mere technicality.

Mike could at least tinkle a few ivories, and he also had access to his brother's guitar and amp, plus that other band essential, a van. They were also allowed to rehearse in the Barson's house so it was obvious that he would be the leader of this little combo. Meanwhile Lee got hold of a clarinet which he soon swapped for a knocked-off saxophone. He had his first and last lesson at Highbury School, but never went back because the teacher noticed that the sax's serial number had been filed off. Still, Lee was out of work as often as he was in it, so had plenty of time to practise.

Chrissy Boy's dad was actually a well-known folk singer and had tried to teach his son the guitar a few years before, but Chris wasn't having any of it. He got around his lack of musical knowledge by doing as Mike told him and by only playing one string at a time. A £20 tax rebate got him his first guitar after Lee told him where one was going cheap. Probably because Lee had changed the price tag on it.

They might not have been accomplished musicians, but punk rock it wasn't. While the Pistols and The Clash were spitting out safety pin anthems, here were three likely lads playing along to a stolen Fats Domino LP. What's more, they were soon joined by

"I did have a few classical lessons, but most of what I know I taught myself during those sessions."

Barso

Overleaf: The North London Invaders' first gig in Si Birdsall's back garden. The picture is taken from the film *Take It Or Leave It*, in which John Hasler (seen here playing drums) appeared as himself. (Stiff/GTO)

another friend, John Hasler, who became the band's drummer, and a certain Carl Smyth, who did a window cleaning round with Lee and who agreed to learn the bass.

Carl was another of life's outsiders. As a child he had moved about a lot, living in his family's native Ireland as well as England and even Iran for a while, and he missed a lot of schooling. He became a skinhead when Lee offered him money to have a crop. A friend, Si Birdsall, had to have one following injuries received during a fight with greasers at a Bazooka Joe concert in Haverstock Town Hall, and Lee wanted a few of the boys to show some solidarity with him. Bazooka Joe for all you trivia fans, were Adam Ant's first band and they played old classics like *Teenager In Love* and *Apache* as well as their own tunes. Singer with the band was none other than Danny Barson, Mike's other brother. They also gave The Sex Pistols their first gig, but that's another story for somebody else's book. Carl's alter ego was a certain Chas Smash, a name picked up from a postcard Hasler had sent him from a not so far away holiday destination.

There's nothing quite like a baptism of fire to get rid of the cobwebs, and so the band got themselves their first gig on 30th

Above: The Invaders at Acklam Hall, 1978, as portrayed in Take It Or Leave It (Stiff/GTO)

June 1977. Si Birdsall said they could play at his party in a big house in Compton Terrace, Islington. They called themselves The North London Invaders and ended up having to play in the back garden. In fact they carried the piano down to ground level so they could use it, and to this day it has never gone back up the stairs.

All that was missing in the line-up was someone to exercise his tonsils. The job was given to another acquaintance, an American actor with the unlikely name of Dikron who happened to be the brother of one of Mike's girlfriends. It was Dikron's job to learn the words to their set, but even with the help of an Elvis Presley songbook, the boy screwed up. Nobody would probably have been any the wiser if all had gone to plan, but it was too dark in the garden for him to read any of the words, and so he was sacked on the spot. He couldn't sing anyway, and the band ended up playing a set of instrumentals. *Swan Lake, I'm Walkin', Lover Please, Just My Imagination, For Once In My Life, It's Too Late* and *The Roadette Song* was how it all began. By all accounts they were dreadful, and most people didn't even bother coming down stairs to see them perform, but at least one partygoer liked them. And as fate would have it that person just happened to be Suggs McPherson.

Now depending on what teeny rag legend you believe, Suggs was either overheard singing on a bus or after a night out at the flicks, but either way he was asked to audition as vocalist. The day of the rehearsal, Suggs got pissed with his mate Andrew "Chalky" White on a bottle of vodka, and ended up singing the only song he knew all of the words to, *See You Later Alligator*. Nobody else was auditioning for the job so that was all he had to do to clinch it.

Before their first proper gig at the City And East in February, 1978, both Chas and Lee had been shown the door. Whether they jumped or were pushed depends on who you talk to. Certainly things were starting to get serious - John Hasler had even put words to one of Mike's songs, *Mistakes* - but holding a band together when musical ability wasn't exactly at a premium, isn't the easiest of tasks. Chas left after falling out with Barso when a promised lift home after rehearsals one night never materialised. Lee also left after one clash too many with Barso, but replacements weren't too hard to find.

Gavin Rogers, the brother of another of Barso's ex-girlfriends, came in on bass, and he was accompanied by the sister of one of Chris' old schoolmates, Lucinda Garland, who played sax. The City And East was to be her one and only gig because she was soon to leave for University, and that opened the door for Lee again. Problem was his family had moved to Luton and he started missing some rehearsals. He did make it to the band's next outing at The Nightingale off Park Road, but then left the band again. He still kept in touch and turned up at rehearsals from time to time, but he actually started playing in another band closer to home called Gilt Edge.

Personnel problems continued when Suggs left after being given the choice between practising with the band or going to watch his beloved Chelsea. Since it was the football season, Stamford Bridge won hands down over the rehearsal room off Finchley Road. John Hasler was chosen to replace him on the sole grounds that he knew the words to the songs. The fact that he couldn't sing didn't seem to matter because he hadn't been much better at playing the

"We realised it could work when we wrote our first song, Mistakes. Until then we'd mucked about playing reggae and rock n' roll at parties."
Chrissy Boy

13

drums. Gavin Rogers threw in the towel too because of the band's near total lack of organisation.

That left two positions to fill. One of Hasler's friends, Mark "Bedders" Bedford came in on bass. He was a big Motown fan and had played in a band that did mostly Beatles' covers. And as luck would have it, he knew a man by the name of Garry Dovey who could keep time with the sticks. Even better, Bedders was still at school, and as a member of the William Ellis Secondary School Common Room Committee he managed to get The North London Invaders a gig at the end of year dance. July 3rd was the big day, and the band picked up the princely sum of one hundred pounds to help pay for the lights and amps.

Surprising though it was, not least to the members of the band, the very same line-up managed to get another gig under their collective belt, at the 3 C's Club in Warren Street. All good things must come to an end however, and Lee returned that Autumn - not to play live, but to thump Garry Dovey. Musical differences they call it, but it was enough to send Dovey packing.

Fortunately, Bedders knew another drummer by the name of Daniel "Woody" Woodgate. They occasionally jammed together in a heavy metal band called Steel Erection, and Woody had actually been at the William Ellis gig and later said the Invaders sounded, "dreadful but brilliant, really rough". He had heard through the grapevine that the Invaders needed a drummer and that they wanted him to join. So he 'phoned Bedders, only to be told that Bedders hadn't even thought of asking him!

With friends like that . . . but since they didn't have anyone else in mind, Woody was invited along to the next rehearsal. Woody, by his own admission, was a bit of a hippy and was well into clever dick music, but as long as he could bang out a tune on the drums he was exactly what the Invaders were looking for.

Things still weren't as they should be. Hasler on vocals just wasn't working out and try though he did, he had about as much talent in the singing stakes as an alley cat. Bedders was working at a roller blind factory called Blind Alley at the time, and the boss threw a party and asked the band to play at it. John Hasler was away on holiday so Chrissy Boy asked Suggs to stand in and he jumped at the chance. That gig saw the first performance of *My Girl* (then called *The New Song*) with Mike singing it, and in the audience was a certain Lee Thompson who kept shouting, "Where's the sax player?".

Even when he wasn't in the band, Suggsy always turned up at gigs, but it was obvious that the band were still looking for a more reliable frontman when Suggs spotted an ad in the back of *Melody Maker*, saying that The Invaders were looking for a professional singer! He pretended he hadn't seen it, and kept turning up for rehearsals. In fact one of the times he ended up playing drums! Hasler meanwhile was given the role of getting the band gigs and given the title of manager.

It was really the beginning of the end for Hasler as far as the band was concerned. He had tried his hand at both the drums and vocals, but was left behind when the others progressed. Even so, without John Hasler there might never have been a Madness. He

"Suddenly I was in the middle of all these blokes who were older than me and acting like complete maniacs! It was really unnerving!"

Bedders

"I remember my mum saying, 'You've got to get rid of that singer - he's terrible!'."

Woody

Above: Lee and Bedders from the video for *Bed And Breakfast Man*, (Stiff)

was the link between the band's core and the group of blokes Suggs kicked about with, and it was Hasler who knew Bedders too. Never has one man done so much for so many and all that.

Before the end of '78 he had got them a few gigs, including one at Middlesex Poly, and a support slot with reggae band The Tribesmen, and punk band The Valves, at West London's Acklam Hall. Thanks to a local skinhead firm, they were lucky to get out of the Acklam alive, but a few friendly faces were in the crowd that night, including Chas Smash. And it is said that it was there that the nutty dance was born. Both Chas' parents were expert Irish dancers, but the man that was to launch a thousand dance steps hadn't started moving his feet until he was seventeen. "When you've had a few bevvies you have to move about don't you?", he once said.

"Once all the instruments were taken up nobody else could be in the band."

Barso

1979 arrived and The Invaders kicked off the new year with a gig at the London Film Makers Co-Op. Lee was back, and the line-up that we now all know and love as Madness was complete. The name change came about because another band called The Invaders was doing the rounds and they had got themselves a record deal and the extra publicity that went with it. Anyway, The North London Invaders or even the plain old Invaders didn't really suit the sound that the band were now churning out. Other names came and went, including The Soft Shoe Shufflers and The Big Dippers, and they were even called Morris & The Minors for a while,

Overleaf: Madness rehearsal from *Take It Or Leave It* (Stiff/GTO)

15

but the band weren't gigging so the names never even left the rehearsal rooms.

By April they had all agreed on only one name suggested by Chris. It came from a song in their set that they had found on the B side of Prince Buster's classic single, *One Step Beyond*. The band's new name was to be Madness, and madness it was. Total madness. They celebrated with a gig supporting Sore Throat at The Music Machine, and that night Chas actually got up on stage and danced with the band for the first time. Things were really starting to come together.

May 3rd, 1979, the night Margaret Thatcher got elected, Madness played the Hope & Anchor, a stalwart of the London pub circuit and centre of the nutty universe thanks to a juke box stuffed full of Prince Buster and other band favourites. They had been after a gig there for ages, and when they had nothing better to do that's where you were most likely to find them. One such night, Lee, Suggs and Carl turned up for a Rock Against Racism gig. A band from Coventry, The Special AKA, were on the bill and when they started to play, the Madness trio couldn't believe their ears. Here was a band based a hundred miles away up the M1, a band they had never even heard of, and they were playing a similar style of music to Madness. This was too good to be true, so afterwards Suggs got talking to the Special AKA's keyboard player, Jerry Dammers, and it emerged that they knew nothing of Madness either.

The night came to an end and because Dammers had nowhere to kip, Suggs offered to put his new friend up for the night. Dammers said he'd started his own record label called 2 Tone and The Special AKA's debut single, *Gangsters*, was all set for release through Rough Trade. He also asked Madness to support The Special AKA at the Nashville on June 8th and they jumped at the chance. The only problem was that the Nashville date clashed with Madness' first gig at Camden's Dublin Castle. They had been after a gig at the Castle for donkey's years, and only got this one after saying they were a jazz band. Both gigs were important, and in true Madness style they managed to play both. Just.

After leaving the Nashville before The Special AKA had even been on, and making it to The Dublin Castle by the skin of their teeth, Lee asked Chas to introduce the band, and Chas came up with the now famous "Hey you! Don't watch that! Watch this!" routine. The only problem was the band couldn't get him off the stage afterwards, and one reason for his frantic dancing was to stop the others from catching hold of him to throw him off. Still, it was certainly entertaining stuff and Chas became the band's unofficial Master Of Ceremonies and chief nutty dancer from then onwards.

All this talk about a nutty sound came from Lee's assertion that their all the fun of the fair sound couldn't be anything else. This was the musical version of jumping trains to Southend, kiss-me-quick hats, Big Dippers, saucy seaside postcards and goldfish in plastic bags. And with a name like Madness their music just had to be nutty.

The Special AKA were creating the biggest buzz in London since The Sex Pistols, and hundreds had to be turned away from

"We met the nutty boys at one of our first gigs in London - they had a dance which consisted of head-butting each other."

Jerry Dammers

"We were terrible that night at the Dublin Castle, absolutely terrible - we got a three month residency."

Suggs

"The nutty sound's something that Lee Thompson thought up. It's 'cos our music sounds like fairgrounds and organs and things. It just sounds nutty."

Chrissy Boy

that Nashville gig. So three weeks later both bands found themselves back there playing to another packed house. By then, The Specials as they were now known, had signed to Chrysalis and had taken the 2 Tone

Tone label with them. The deal was that 2 Tone would be allowed to record ten songs a year and Chrysalis was obliged to release at least six of them. The budget for each single was just £1,000, a small sum to pay to secure the signatures of Dammers and Co.

It was about time Madness went into the studio to get a demo together and they managed to talk Clive Langer into producing it for them over a few beers. Clive had been in Deaf School, a band that the Madness boys often went to see, and was now pursuing a solo career and working in production. Even better, he had fallen in love with one of the band's numbers, *My Girl*. With what money they could scrape together, the band was booked into the tiny Pathway Studios in Highbury where Elvis Costello had somehow managed to cut an album. Luckily, Elvis didn't have to rely on Woody turning up or else he might never have done it.

Woody actually drove past the studios five times on his motorbike, but never made it to the recording session. Time is money as the saying goes, and there was no point wasting any more of either waiting for Barry Sheene to stick his head around the door. So the band cut their losses and another date was booked, but this time Clive had to go and ask a friend, music publisher Rob Dickens, to put £200 up for the recording.

Eventually three tracks were captured in the studio. There was *The Prince*, Lee's tribute to Prince Buster and all things Blue Beat, *Madness* (natch), and *My Girl*, which had not only been written

Below: Bedders, Chrissy Boy and Barso at The Dublin Castle (Stiff/GTO)

Barso, but was still being sung by him too. No time was wasted getting the tape and a makeshift press release off to 2 Tone, and Madness became the label's first signing, with the band's debut single all set to be *The Prince* backed by *Madness*. The recording of *My Girl* with Mike Barson on vocal duty was put to one side, but later appeared on the 12" of *Return Of The Los Palmas 7*, with Barso billed as The Prince. It might well have ended up on the flip side of *The Prince*, but with it being only a one single deal, nobody wanted to give two original tunes away.

"They sent me this tape which was really dodgy, but had a lot of potential. I don't believe any other record label would have signed them except for 2 Tone."

Jerry Dammers

The single was pencilled in for release on August 10th, and the weeks running up to D-Day saw Madness play their biggest gigs to date. On July 21st, they played the newly sound-proofed Electric Ballroom along with The Specials and The Selecter. 1,500 people turned up for what was billed as a 2 Tone Evening, and the queues

A crowd shot from an early Madness gig. Far left, in hat and crombie, is Gaz Mayall who ran a stall during the 2 Tone days selling skinhead-related clothes. He later graduated on to the club scene with Gaz's Rockin' Blues, and to having his own ska label which launched The Potato 5's recording career, as well as that of his own band, The Trojans.

threatened to block Camden High Street on a number of occasions before the doors opened. Talk about a carnival atmosphere. *Gangsters* was on the verge of a Top Thirty place and it was obvious to anyone there that night that this was the start of something big. The night ended with The Specials being joined on the heaving stage by Madness, The Selecter and half the audience for a knees-up to The Pioneers' classic slice of skinhead reggae, *Long Shot Kick De Bucket*.

Then on July 29th, Madness played the Lyceum for the first time as guests of The Pretenders. They were rehearsing for this gig at the Archway studios when they first saw the newly pressed and bagged single, *The Prince*. "It was like a football team winning the F.A. Cup, it was great!", said Suggs of the celebrations that followed. Nearly all bands dream of the day they make it on to vinyl, and for Madness it was no different. To them Christmas had come six months early.

On the day the single was released, Madness played the Dublin Castle. *Melody Maker* hit the nail on the head when they said, "No juke box should be without a copy", and within a few weeks it's unlikely that one was. The band then went on the road to promote the single, concentrating on the London pubs and clubs, but making it as far afield as Liverpool Eric's. Pick of the bunch was the bank holiday gig at the Lyceum on 26th of August, with Secret Affair, The Purple Hearts, The Selecter and The Little Roosters. *Quadrophenia* was still showing at cinemas up and down the country, and the gig was packed with skins and mods who the following day would be heading for the seaside for bank holiday battles with the teds.

A further boost had come in the shape of a John Peel session for Radio One which was recorded on the 14th of August and first broadcast the night after the Lyceum gig. It featured a different version of *The Prince, Bed And Breakfast Man, Land Of Hope And Glory* (with Lee on vocals) and *Stepping Into Line*. And for anyone who missed it, the four tracks were released on the Strange Fruit label in 1986 as part of their excellent series of Peel Sessions.

Despite John Peel's support, the rave reviews and the 2 Tone seal of approval, *The Prince* took its time to make its mark and it didn't enter the charts until September 1st. It eventually spent eleven weeks in the charts, peaking at number sixteen on October 2nd. The week it entered the Dirty Thirty, the band sat in the 2 Tone office above Holt's the shoe shop in Camden, waiting to hear if they would be on *Top Of The Pops*. It was touch and go, but Secret Affair got the spot in the end with *Time For Action*. Still, there was no stopping the band now, and they made it on to the box with *The Prince* the following week. No thanks to Chrysalis though, who stopped promoting the single once Madness had decided to take their business elsewhere.

"The old record labels have no insight and the only reason half of them go after a band is because someone else is going after them. If someone's interested in you, they're all interested in you."

Suggs

With all the talk of a ska revival and the success of The Specials, other labels were trying to get their slice of the chequered cake. A lot of the major labels were after Madness with Island, Virgin and Elton John's Rocket label leading the pack, alongside Chrysalis. It was no doubt very flattering to the band to know they were in such demand, but it would have been even nicer if some of the interested parties had wanted Madness for Madness' sake and not just because they knew everyone else wanted to sign them. One first class plonker didn't even know that the band had a single in the charts. During talks with Madness he had to send his secretary out to get it! The funniest thing about this though was that the A&R man in question was from Chrysalis and his secretary only had to go to another department in the same building to grab a copy.

At the start of September, the band decided to sign on the dotted line with Stiff Records. Any label that had Ian Dury & The Blockheads on its roster couldn't be all bad, and at least Madness got to talk to the label's boss, Dave Robinson, and not a string of monkeys who had to clear everything with an elusive organ grinder. Some of the clowns who were sent to court Madness had to ask permission to wipe their own arses.

Dave Robinson had just got married and on his return from the honeymoon in Nassau, he arranged a bash at the Clarendon Ballroom. He wanted to see Madness for himself and so coughed up two hundred notes for them to play at his party. He was obviously impressed by what he saw, and from then on went all out to secure the band for Stiff

Staying with 2 Tone was never really on the cards. There was no provision in the 2 Tone deal for albums, other than by The Specials who were committed to supplying five LPs. Madness for their part were desperate to record an album, and Stiff were just as keen. If things had been different though, and they had stayed with 2 Tone, there was every chance that their debut album would have been ready for release before The Specials had *Specials* in the shops.

"They came to take the piss, but I thought they were wonderful. They even got Elvis Costello to dance, which is a thing you don't often do. They literally dragged him on to the floor!"

Dave Robinson

Also, there was a real danger that Madness would always play second fiddle to The Specials if they stayed with 2 Tone. After all the Coventry band did own the label, at least in name. In fact, The Selecter were soon given equal say in the label's affairs which could have seen Madness' interests demoted further.

Madness didn't fall out with Jerry Dammers over the move or anything. In fact they remained the best of friends. It was just that if they were going to make it big time, it would be on their own terms. So they bid farewell to the good ship 2 Tone and prepared for a voyage of a lifetime with Stiff Records at the helm.

ONE STEP BEYOND

THE remainder of September was taken up with a handful of gigs and by going into the studio to record an album. Getting the album together was a lot easier than might be imagined because it was basically the set the band had been refining for two years. Stiff were anxious to get the album out while there was so much interest in 2 Tone related bands, and within three weeks, *One Step Beyond,* had been recorded and mixed, and the cover artwork was ready for the printers.

To promote the album, Madness agreed to play the forthcoming 2 Tone Tour with The Specials and The Selecter. As a warm-up to that though, Madness set off in a van to play ten dates in England, starting off at Warwick University on October 2nd and finishing at Brighton Poly on the 13th.

Already, the band's reputation of being a skinhead band was attracting more than its fair share of trouble. At Huddersfield on the 6th, a coachload of fans from Middlesbrough were refused entry to a student gig and a small riot erupted. The van Madness were using was trashed, as was the one carrying the film crew that was in tow at the time to record a video for their first Stiff single. Then two days later at Oldham Civic Hall, routine security checks found fans turning up at the gig with blades, and one nutter even brought a home-made mace with him!

On the 12th, Madness headlined the Electric Ballroom for the first time, with Bad Manners and Echo & The Bunnymen in support. It was their biggest London gig to date, with smaller venues like the Hope & Anchor no longer able to cope with the swelling ranks of the Madness army. Manners started the night off, and their brand of ska n' blues went down well enough in front of Madness' home crowd. No such luck for The Bunnymen though. They went down like a lead balloon, mainly because the punters had come to see ska bands and this outfit didn't even come close. Skinheads prevented them from completing their set, and Suggsy's half-hearted attempts to calm things down came to nothing. In the end, only the appearance of Madness on stage was enough to pacify the restless natives.

It was more a reflection of the times than anything to do with Madness though. All sorts of gigs kicked off over everything from the length of your hair to a spilt drink. Much of the trouble was football related as rival fans turned dancefloors into battlefields, and extremist politics reared its ugly head to add fuel to the flames. The end result was that a lot of people were going to all sorts of gigs looking for a punch-up, and not surprisingly they usually ended up finding one.

After Brighton, it was off to London's Roundhouse for three days of beer and rehearsals along with The Specials and The Selecter. Then on October 19th, a coach pulled up, all three bands piled on, and it was back to Brighton for the first night of the tour. In true rock n' roll fashion, the bands got to the Top Rank late and both Madness and The Selecter suffered from rushed

"The 2 Tone Tour was great, but it had to be the last time it could be that chaotic and hectic."

Suggs

Right: Chas Smash in action
(Stiff/Michael Putland)

24

soundchecks. It was still a great night and nobody in the audience seemed any the wiser as they danced the night away, sweating buckets as they did so.

And so the tour continued. The 2 Tone coach would pull into town with the Madness crew making all the noise, the bands would set up stall, and that evening they would spread the gospel according to ska. The media coverage at the time guaranteed full houses up and down the country. Radio, TV, the music press, even the tabloids, were full of stuff on the bands and it was as if a black and white blanket was covering the British Isles. And as far as the sharpest kids were concerned, that's exactly what was happening.

Things hotted up even more towards the end of October when both The Specials and Madness released their debut albums in the same week. *One Step Beyond* featured fifteen favourites from the live set, including *Madness* which was not noted on the sleeve for some reason. Except on some foreign releases anyway. That and the title track were covers from the same Prince Buster single, but the only other borrowed tunes were traditional songs injected with some nutty flair, the best of which being *Swan Lake*. Other tracks of note were later to appear as singles, but even today the album deserves to be dusted down at regular intervals to give

"The British 2 Tone Tour that we did with The Specials and The Selecter was the best I've ever been involved in. We thought that we were doing something good and it was really exciting. We were having the time of our lives."

Chas

almost forgotten gems like *Believe Me*, *Mummy's Boy,* and *In The Middle Of The Night* an airing. Superb stuff all round.

The sleeve's front cover featured the band doing the now infamous nutty train and the back saw Chas Smash demonstrating his fancy footwork in a series of black and white stills. He wasn't a full member of the band at the time, but was credited on the sleeve for his backing vocals and various shouts. In fact it was Chas and his brother Brendan who were responsible for the accapello *Chipmunks Are Go* on the tail end of side two. The inner sleeve featured a collage of passport photos that fans were asked to send in, and also allowed Chalky, Toks, Totts, Whets and Prince Nutty, collectively better known as the away team, to get their ugly mugs on the album. In fact, the staff at London Underground were so impressed by the collage that they named a station on the Northern Line after Totts and Whets. Probably.

The following week both *One Step Beyond* and *Specials* entered the charts, but it was the nutty sound that was to come out on top in the long run. It stayed in the charts for an incredible 78 weeks, reached number two and earned the band their first platinum disc (for sales in excess of one million copies), while *Specials* peaked at number four. Obviously the move to Stiff hadn't done our Camden Town boys any harm at all and a year later, when the 2 Tone media backlash was in full force, it was seen as an inspired move. It allowed Madness to progress and thrive, while others fell by the wayside.

On the same day as *One Step Beyond* the album was released, *One Step Beyond* the single came out too. The sort of coincidence you don't come across twice in a lifetime. The single also featured the boys doing the nutty train and the photo was from the same session, only this time appearing in colour. Another way of telling the single and album apart was that the single came in a smaller sleeve. On the B side of the 7", *Mistakes*, made an appearance. It was one of the first songs the band had ever written way back when and it had beginners written all over it, but as well as filling a gap in the Madness story, it also demonstrated just how far the band had come in a relatively short time.

Funnily enough, the band hadn't wanted *One Step Beyond* to be released as a single. It was Dave Robinson's idea. Like most young bands, Madness thought they would have the last say on everything down to the silly messages people scratch on the run-out groove, but the reality was often quite different. Robinson first heard the song when he went along to see how the album was progressing and immediately wanted it to be the first Stiff single. The problem was, it was only a minute long and the band had already called it a day and gone home.

Clive Langer had been kept on after the success of *The Prince* and he was joined at the mixing desks for the album by his mate Alan Winstanley who was by now an experienced producer, having worked with punk bands like The Stranglers, Generation X and 999. In fact he was producing The Stranglers' *Raven* LP when Clive gave him a ring about this great new band from North London.

Anyway, only Clive and Alan were still at the studio when Dave Robinson came up with the new single idea and he asked

"We started off with the intention of designing our own bags and everything, 'cos we're all quite artistic. Suddenly though, you're on tour in Glasgow, and the single's out in London, and it seems we never make time to do anything."

Suggs

Above: A rare photo of Dave Robinson (far right) as he talks to members of the band during the filming of *Take It Or Leave It* **(Stiff).**

so late, they just repeated what had been recorded, so that halfway through, the song came to an end and then started from the beginning again.

Langer and Winstanley only meant it to be a guide to what an extended version would sound like, but by the time they saw Dave Robinson to ask him what he thought of it, the Stiff boss had sent it off to be cut and mastered, ready for pressing! To him, it was always going to be a definite hit and he persuaded the band, against their better judgement, that this should be their next 7". It turned out to be a number seven hit and stayed in the charts for fourteen weeks, longer than any other Madness single bar *Baggy Trousers*.

Back to the tour. After just a week on the road, serious trouble erupted at Hatfield Polytechnic. A gang of around 30 blokes, who had previously been refused entry, burst into the bar through a fire exit and started slashing people with razors and Stanley knives. They were carrying banners announcing their arrival as the Hatfield Mafia and Hatfield Anti-Fascist League, and they made it clear that they were after National Front supporters. Inevitably, a number of innocent bystanders were attacked too, and the final score was ten hospitalised, eleven arrested and a grand's worth of damage done. The fighting took place in a room adjacent to where The Selecter were playing and they continued their set oblivious to what was happening.

Left: Lee and Suggs getting plastered during *Take It Or Leave It* **(Stiff/GTO)**

It wasn't the first violent incident on the tour and it wasn't the last either, but it was certainly the worst. Everyone on the tour tried to play it down as a one-off incident, but more than anything it served to focus media attention on the racist element that was appearing at nearly every ska gig. Again it was hardly the bands' fault and the majority of people turning up weren't the least bit interested in extremist politics, but the media was more interested in sensation than reality, and it gave the far right more publicity than they could have ever wished for.

Both the National Front and British Movement had targetted youth cults for some time, especially in London, and they enjoyed considerable success in doing so. And these same kids saw little contradiction in turning up to see bands playing what was essentially black music. Few actually thought it through because only a committed minority took it seriously. Most kids wearing NF badges did it because it was the thing to do, like bunking off double Maths or smoking behind the bike sheds, and not because they had read every word of the National Front manifesto and were committed lifetime supporters.

Nevertheless fingers started pointing at the bands involved with The 2 Tone Tour. One newspaper even accused The Selecter of being racist, a band in which only Neol Davies was actually white. But when the flak really started to fly it was usually in the direction of Madness. They were the only all-white band on the tour and had the biggest skinhead following to boot. Add those two facts together and it was enough for sections of the media to hang, draw and quarter the band. *The Sunday Times* did an article on racism at gigs which said that Madness were once called the North London Skinhead Elite and it made great play of the fact that both the Young National Front and the British Movement actively recruited at their gigs.

The band couldn't change the colour of their skin. They were born that way and short of painting a few of them black, nothing was going to alter that fact. And the reason they attracted more than their fair share of skinheads was because they were from London where the cult was at its biggest. As Chas said at the time, "A lot of skinheads see us as a home team, a home band".

Unfortunately, that's not all he said though. In an interview with *New Musical Express*, a few throwaway sentences were blown out of all proportion to suggest that Madness didn't mind racists turning up at their gigs. He wasn't even officially in the band at the time, and Madness were quick to distance themselves from what he had said, issuing a press statement saying, "There's no way any of us are fascists - we are categorically against it".

The truth was that Madness as a band weren't even interested in politics. The Stiff t-shirts proclaiming Fuck Art - Let's Dance, summed Madness up perfectly. But at the same time, they had grown up on the same streets as those coming to their gigs and didn't want to turn their backs on them. If they had done, it might have pleased a handful of journalists, but it would also have alienated the kids further.

Members of other bands, including The Beat's Rankin' Roger and The Specials' Lynval Golding, saw more merit in having racists at their gigs where they could see black and white people sharing the same stage. Certainly, the appearance of The Specials,

"All that bloody right-wing stuff is just fashion. One week they're in the NF, the next it's BM. If you try to have an intelligent conversation about it, they've no idea what you're talking about."

Barso

"We don't care if the crowd are in the NF or BM or whatever as long as they behave themselves, having a good time and not fighting. What does it matter? Who cares what their political views are? We don't ask them if they're Conservative or Labour when they come through the door. There's no difference, they're all kids."

Chas

If we wanted to talk about politics, we'd have formed a debating society, not a fucking band."

Suggs

2 TONE TOUR

OCT. 31 HANLEY Victoria Hall
NOV. 1 BLACKBURN Golden Palms
2 LANCASHIRE University
4 SHEFFIELD Top Rank
5 LEICESTER De Montfort Hall
6 PORTSMOUTH Guild Hall
7 CARDIFF Top Rank
8 DERBY Kings Hall
9 NEWCASTLE (Venue to be confirmed)

OCT. 19 BRIGHTON Top Rank
20 SWINDON Oasis
21 BOURNEMOUTH Stateside Center
22 EXETER University
23 PLYMOUTH Fiesta
26 NORWICH University of East Anglia
27 HATFIELD Poly
28 WOLVERHAMPTON Civic Hall
29 BIRMINGHAM Top Rank

NOV. 10 STIRLING University
11 GLASGOW (Venue to be confirmed)
12 EDINBURGH Tiffanys
13 ABERDEEN Ruffles
14 AYR Pavilion
15 CARLISLE Market Hall
16 LEEDS University
17 LOUGHBOROUGH University

NOV. 18 BRISTOL Locarno
21 LIVERPOOL Mountford Hall
22 DUBLIN Olympic Ballroom*
23 BELFAST University*
25 LONDON Lyceum
26 HEMEL HEMSTEAD Pavilion
28 CLEETHORPES Winter Gardens
29 COVENTRY Tiffanys

THE SPECIALS
MADNESS THE SELECTER
DEXY'S MIDNIGHT RUNNERS

*Specials & Dr. Feelgood only
From 15 Nov. onwards Dexy's Midnight Runners will replace Madness.

31

Madness and The Selecter on the same episode of *Top Of The Pops* in November did as much for anti-racism as any other event that year.

Madness left the 2 Tone Tour after the five Scottish dates, but talk that they were forced to leave because of their following was absolute rubbish.   From day one it was advertised that after November 14th, Dexy's Midnight Runners would be replacing them and that's exactly what happened.   The nutty boys then played a few extra dates, including another at the Electric Ballroom where support band Red Beans & Rice came in for the hard time.   Then Madness boarded a plane to the United States for their first taste of touring on the other side of the Big Pond.

Above: Bedders during the filming of the video for *It Must Be Love* (Stiff)

When they signed to Stiff they had made a similar deal with Sire in the States and were desperate to get out there before The Specials made it. The only problem was that Sire wouldn't release the album so close to Christmas and Madness arrived in a country where few people had even heard of them.   They ended up playing a few low-key dates, with Chas Smash now a full-time member of the band, and then headed back to London in time for the release of *My Girl* on December 21st.

Putting out a single four days before Christmas Day virtually screamed commercial suicide, but the band had wanted this to be the first Stiff single and the label were happy to see it go out before the end of 1979. It entered the charts at the start of the new year, with Madness performing it on the first *Top Of The Pops* of 1980, and against the odds it ended up in the number three spot. It was also the band's first number one if you lived in France, which just goes to show what good taste the frogs have. The flip side of *My Girl* was another one from the band's vaults, *Stepping Into Line*, and the 12" had *In The Rain* on it too. In fact quite a few of the 12" singles were given away with the *One Step Beyond* album in selected retail outlets.

It was actually very close to being the band's last single. All the violence and politics at gigs was getting to them, and there was a real danger that Madness would end up being crucified by sections of their following just as Sham 69 had been that summer. John Hasler, the band's manager, summed up Madness' feelings at the time by saying, "The band aren't in a position to issue an ultimatum as that just might encourage people to wreck gigs, but I would think that if it got really heavy, they would jack it in".

Fortunately, it didn't come to that, and January, 1980, saw the band jet-setting off again, this time for a series of European appearances. Then it was back to Old Blighty to play a gig each in Liverpool, Glasgow, Birmingham and London. By now, the music press were taking a closer look at the band and reviewers often criticised their musical ability. True, Suggsy's voice wasn't the greatest The Shed has ever heard, and none of the others were looking to win Musician Of The Year. But nobody was going to Madness gigs for musical perfection. This was dance music and everyone, except the odd reviewer, was too busy moving their feet to notice one or two bum notes.

On Saturday 16th of February, Madness played London's Hammersmith Odeon, but this was to be a gig with a difference. Not only was it a morning gig, scotching the rumour that pop stars never get up before midday, but entry was also restricted to their younger fans. Tickets went on sale three weeks before at a pound a piece and sold out the same day, leaving hundreds of ticketless fans to be turned away on the morning of the show.

To underline their commitment to their younger fans, a junior press conference was held afterwards, with the pop press being represented by pint-size reporters. For some strange reason most of the questions revolved around the type of underwear the boys wore, and so as not to disappoint anyone, band members displayed their boxer shorts with pride.

They just about had time to catch their breath before heading off to Uncle Sam's again. This time they stayed five weeks and although they got to play larger venues, the tour was pure hell. The Specials were in the U.S. at the same time, although they weren't gigging with Madness, and both bands had a hard time of it. The sheer size of the place and the monotonous travelling between gigs have been the ruin of many a fine band, and two more casualties were almost added to the list.

The Specials actually played a lot of the same venues as Madness, although usually a week or so later. That gave the Maddies ample opportunity to leave rude messages about The Specials all over the walls of various dressing rooms, knowing full

"We're only in this game for a laugh and if we are forced to drop out then none of us would have any regrets at all. We don't want anything to do with the National Front. As far as I'm concerned, if they start venting their political feelings at our gigs, then we can call it a day."

Thommo

"When it's all kids they go completely loony. They've got no preconceptions or ideas about being super cool. They're just great gigs."

Suggs

"When you play somewhere like Portland, Oregon, it's all pointless. During our set everyone was playing pool and songs get lost against the sinking eight balls."

Bedders

33

well that the Coventry boys would be along in a few days to read them.

Both bands played New York within nights of each other and in many ways the Big Apple summed up their respective tours. The Specials played the Diplomat Hotel Ballroom on March 1st, but the ten dollar ticket price was high even by American standards. Articles even appeared in the local press about it, and about a week before the gig, official looking posters started appearing all over the city. About the same time as Madness came to town funnily enough.

Anyway, these hoax posters took the form of an open letter supposedly from The Specials. It apologised for the high ticket prices and said that 500 free tickets had been put aside for "our poorer fans". To claim a ticket all you had to do was 'phone any of the four numbers listed below. And there they were for all to ring - the promoter's office and home 'phone number, the booking agent's number and the number for the head of Chrysalis. Needless to say, all four lines were pretty busy during the days leading up to the gig.

Madness had no such problems shifting tickets for what was a similar sized venue. In fact they could have filled it twice, but the stress of touring and living in each others pockets for so long had taken its toll. The band were all at each other's throats and Thommo ended up throwing a wobbly, not to mention a few chairs,

Below: Members of Madness and The Specials herald the return of the rude boy cult.

in the packed dressing room. It certainly shifted the hangers-on anyway.

No sooner had they got back from the States and Stiff had them doing a fortnight worth of dates on the Continent. Not that their record label had been idle while they swanned about America though. Stiff had pressed and packaged *Work, Rest And Play* without the band's full knowledge, and it caused a lot of bad feeling between Madness and their label. It was a four track affair featuring *Night Boat To Cairo* from the debut album and three previously unreleased tracks, including Chas Smash's tongue in cheek message to the press, *Don't Quote Me On That*.

The band wanted some of the tracks re-mixed and for the single to be promoted as an EP because they felt the other two tracks, *Deceives The Eye* and *The Young And The Old,* were good songs in their own right. They made a lot of noises, but with the record all set for a March 28th release, there wasn't a lot they could really do except live with it. A week after release, *Work, Rest And Play* was in the charts and it ended up reaching the number six spot.

By the time they had done the European dates, Madness were exhausted and with a family bereavement in the band, the first five dates of their U.K. tour were cancelled. When the tour did get under way, Madness were joined by The Go-Gos, an all female band from Hollywood who had played with the nutty boys on both their jaunts to the U.S., and Clive Langer & The Boxes who had Mike's brother Ben on keyboards.

Reggae great and latest Stiff signing, Desmond Dekker, joined them at the Lyceum too, but all in all the tour was a financial disaster. With the massive support the band now had, Madness could have been filling big venues the length and breadth of the British Isles, but instead they chose to play smaller venues in towns where major tours rarely ventured.

It was great for those fans who would otherwise never have seen their heroes, but it ended up costing the band a small fortune.

The tour continued until June, with Lee's cousin Vince doing the business at gigs with nutty hats, Madness t-shirts and the like. The poor bloke got so tired and emotional with the job that he finished the tour with a collapsed lung! Then, apart from two nights at Nottingham's Theatre Royal in August which were filmed by ATV, all was relatively quiet on the Madders front until the release of *Baggy Trousers* on September 5th.

1980 had started with Pink Floyd's *Another Brick In The Wall* at number one in the charts. Its anti-school message, with the "we don't need no education" line didn't do anybody any real favours. School might be boring, for both pupils and teachers at times, but the old one about it being the best years of your life generally rings true in the end. And that's where *Baggy Trousers* came in.

To accompany the single, Madness produced the first of their now legendary videos. It was directed by Dave Robinson, who had been a photographer before starting Stiff, and cost only a thousand pounds to make - peanuts for pop videos even then (*One Step Beyond* had cost nine times as much, but you'd never have known). The highlight was Lee flying through the air playing his sax, with an out of sight crane lifting him off the ground. It was an inexpensive stunt, but the final effect was far better than anyone imagined it would be. The single spent four months in the charts, peaking at number three, and went gold.

It was also later used in a TV commercial for Colgate toothpaste, but the ultimate advertisements for Madness singles from *Baggy Trousers* on were their magical three minute videos. By the time the likes of *Wings Of A Dove*, *House Of Fun* and *Cardiac Arrest* had graced TV screens, Madness had video-making down to a fine art. Flying through the air, walking on ceilings, joyriding in double decker buses, throwing a van out of a plane at 20,000 feet. You name it, they tried it.

The other thing about videos was that they attracted more and more young kids to the Madness sound. The matinee shows had been introduced because of the young fans who would always turn up outside venues even if they had no chance of getting a ticket because of age restrictions. And now, with the release of *Baggy Trousers*, even more youngsters were rallying to the cry of Madness. All over the country, kids barely into their teens and younger would sit glued to the box, hoping to learn just a few of Chas Smash's dancesteps to impress their mates down the local youth club.

In the coming months and years, Madness fully realised the importance of their young following and did a great deal to cater for

"On tour there were these vast numbers of kids and sometimes they couldn't get into the gigs. And the irony was that wasn't what we intended to be at all. We were macho and hard and rebels without things."

Suggs

36

it, but the biggest surprise was the change in the media's attitude towards the band. Up until the end of 1979, Madness were seen largely as a street-level band with a hooligan following, but just months into 1980 and all you saw of the band was glossy pull-outs and madcap TV antics. Obviously the band were happy to go along with it all - it helped sell records after all - but the problem was that the serious side to Madness was largely buried in typical pop hype manure. For the time being anyway.

Later that September, the band's second LP, *Absolutely*, hit the shops to the accompaniment of press ads announcing, "The Camden Cowboys Ride Again". It too went straight into the charts, stayed there for 46 weeks and was only kept off the number one spot by The Police. On it was *Baggy Trousers*, as was the single's flip side, although this time with words. The album track was *Take It Or Leave It*, but Clive Langer always thought it would sound good as an instrumental and that's how it ended up on the single under the name of *The Business*.

Two other songs, *Embarrassment* and *Return Of The Los Palmas 7*, were later to be taken from the album too, leading to accusations that Stiff were milking the fans by releasing too many tracks off each album. Of course, Stiff weren't the first label to do that and they weren't the last either, and worse was still to come with more 12" releases, picture discs and so on. What's more Stiff claimed that singles were only released to promote the album, and barely made any money. The 12" of *Return Of The Los Palmas 7* lost 2p a copy according to Dave Robinson. Almost makes you want to send the bloke a tenner.

If singles were such a millstone then it makes you wonder why Stiff went to the expense of releasing the 7" of *Return Of The Los Palmas 7* in two different picture sleeves. The fact that a lot of fans would end up buying both, thereby pushing it further up the charts and putting more money into the label's pockets, probably didn't even enter Robinson's mind.

That same month, Woody married Jane from The Mo-dettes, but things didn't get off to the best of starts. Days later, the bride headed off for a six week tour of the States and returned the very day Woody headed off to the Continent with Madness. Such was life in the crazy world of rock n' roll at the time, and if that wasn't enough, bands were expected to appear on a wild children's TV show by the name of *Tiswas*.

Madness were by now ideal material for *Tiswas* and looked destined to be on it every other week. That was until the fateful day of September 27th, when the nutty boys managed to get themselves and the entire Stiff stable banned from the show. Things started well enough, with Suggs and Chas dressed up as circus clowns, The Co-Co Twins. Then aunt Sally James got squirted in the eye by Suggs. Quite normal behaviour for *Tiswas*, so Sally smiled and he squirted her again. The smile disappeared and Suggs tried to make amends by wiping the cream from her face.

Below: Madness join Mike Reid for a special Christmas edition of the kiddies' TV show, *Runaround*. The programme went out on Christmas Day, 1980, and to get everyone in the festive spirit, the show was done on ice. For all those who remember the show, G-G-G-G-G-Go!

Instead he only managed to poke her one in the eye, removing a false eyelash in the process. Then to cap it all, a kid bit Lee and Lee naturally retaliated. A good day's work done, the lads returned to London by train, with The Co-Co Twins still dressed in their daft costumes, and so ended their *Tiswas* days.

November 14th saw the release of the number four hit, *Embarrassment*, backed by *Crying Shame*, and the band preparing for the 12 Days Of Christmas Tour. A warm up gig took place at the Hope & Anchor in support of Blanket Aid, a charity set up to help London's homeless. The venue's capacity was reduced to a hundred at the time and the gig was really just for family and friends and not advertised.

The December dates included matinee shows at all the gigs bar Glasgow and Henley, with tickets costing a pound instead of the £2.50-£3.00 for the evening gigs. What's more, the first issue of the *Beano*-style *Nutty Boys* comic was distributed at these gigs to great popular acclaim. Future copies were sent free of charge to members of the Madness Information Service (M.I.S. to you) and went on sale at gigs.

The tour finished off with three dates at Hammersmith Odeon. Originally only two were planned for the 22nd and 23rd, with Madness not wanting to play London on Christmas Eve because public transport knocked off early for the festive holidays. However, the band did pencil in a last minute charity show at the Odeon on the 24th. A toy collection was held and come the big day, members of the band distributed the goodies to children's homes.

The year ended on a real high note, with the band being crowned single artists of 1980 thanks to four top ten singles which spent a total of 50 weeks in the charts. They celebrated by playing at Elvis Costello's Christmas Show at the NEC on December 27th with the man himself, UB40 and The Selecter in front of 6,000 people. And on New Years Eve, Suggs and Chas celebrated the coming of 1981 as The Rubber Biscuits at The Venue. Sharing the bill that night was Bette Bright, who was soon to become Mrs. Suggs.

Just when the hangovers were beginning to fade, up popped Stiff with the *Return Of The Los Palmas 7* single. It was not the most obvious choice for 7" treatment, not least because it was an instrumental. It was also released when Madness' previous two singles were still in the Top 75. The B side had *That's The Way To Do It* on it, and it obviously was as it gave the band their sixth Top Ten hit in a row, reaching number seven. Within weeks, Stiff had collected all six singles together in a fold out plastic wallet - just in case you missed one or two of them.

The 12" of *Return Of The Los Palmas 7* had *My Girl* from the band's first demo and a live version of *Swan Lake*, and a lot of copies went out with *The Nutty Boys* comic thrown in for good measure. The band certainly had enough to spare thanks to their new manager, John Kelloggs. He had the bright idea of having 250,000 copies of issue one printed in the belief that they would go on sale in newsagents throughout the country. Years later, the band still had thousands of the bastards left.

In February it was Mike Barson's turn to tie the knot. He married Sandra at Finsbury Park Registry Office and celebrated with a slap up breakfast for two at George's cafe on the Holloway Road. He hadn't even told the rest of the band about it, although he had dropped a subtle hint by saying he would be a bit late for rehearsals that day.

The other big event of that month should have been the release of *Dance Craze*, the film about 2 Tone, but in the end it was a huge disappointment. Jerry Dammers had been working on it for what seemed like ages, and the pressure of it and everything else, caused him to have a nervous breakdown. What with everything else on his plate, time just wasn't on Jerry's side, and the final result fell well short of the mark. Most people were expecting it to be the story of 2 Tone, but it was nothing more than a series of live takes strung together. Madness were well represented with six songs, more than any other band including The Specials, and three of them, *One Step Beyond*, *Night Boat To Cairo* and *Razor Blade Alley*, made it on to the simultaneously released album.

The idea for *Dance Craze* had actually come from American film maker, Joe Massot. He had bumped into Madness at a Los Angeles hotel during their first tour and was totally knocked out by the band when he saw them perform that night. He decided to make a film about Madness, but when his son told him about other ska bands like The Specials, he widened his horizons. During 1980, he went on the road with the bands, and from all the footage shot came the 27 songs that were to be immortalised forever on celluloid.

If it had been released a year earlier it would have been a big box office success, but although the album was a number five chart hit, the film didn't really capture the nation's imagination. 2 Tone was no longer the force it was and those bands who chose to pursue their careers elsewhere - The Beat with Go Feet, UB40 with Graduate, Bad Manners at Magnet and Madness at Stiff - were in a far healthier position than any of those they left behind, with the possible exception of The Specials.

The opportunity to capture something other than live footage would have been completely lost if Madness hadn't decided to make their own film, *Take It Or Leave It*. They were already becoming dab hands at the video game and this was their big chance to extend their talents to a full length feature film. Each member of the band put up £20,000 to make *Take It Or Leave It* and the remainder of the £250,000 budget came from Stiff. It sounds like a lot of money and was certainly a lot to risk, but in film circles it was small change.

The idea was to show Madness in their early years and to demonstrate just how easy it was for anyone to start a band and maybe make it all the way to the top. Dave Robinson was to be director and he also scripted the film. He talked to each band member about the years leading up to the release of *The Prince*, and then put their memories together to form a complete picture. The first script proved to be too expensive, so a few corners were cut and they were ready to start filming on March 9th.

A few things were changed for effect - like Chrissy Boy was never really employed to squeeze big parcels into small boxes - but

Above: Madness prepare for the release of *Embarrassment*, a number four hit for the band (Stiff)

they tried to keep it as close to what actually happened as possible. Madness played themselves as did people connected with the band like John Hasler, and the actor's union, Equity, was kept happy with a sprinkling of genuine actors in the cast. Not that it mattered because the card-carrying members were all given roles that didn't suit them and it just added to the general mayhem.

Some of the original venues were also used, including The Dublin Castle which was booked for the filming of a hush hush gig. The Acklam Hall couldn't be used because of damage caused a few months before when a new punk convention held there had ended in a riot, but the Keskiddee Community Centre played the part beautifully.

The film was in the can by the middle of April. No doubt something of a record for the film industry. It was actually shot on 16mm and then blown up to 35mm to save money. The black and white shots that open the film were originally sent to Sweden for processing, but the lab made a mess of it and when the film came back it was all bleached out. So it was back to square one to reshoot three days worth of filming, but for the most part things went to plan. One of the most surprising outcomes of filming though was to find that seemingly petty arguments over things like a borrowed pair of shoes were still the cause of resentment between members of the band years later.

Take It Or Leave It premiered at Camden Town Gate (where else) on October 14th before opening at Croydon, Romford and Hammersmith ABCs. The press had seen it a week before at the plush BAFTA Theatre in Piccadilly with mixed reactions. They most

"I think that people got the impression that I was being stroppy when all I wanted was to get things done."

Barso

Above: Madness bump into Bow Wow Wow during a visit to Japan (Stiff/Andre Csillag)

probably expected a whacky cartoon-come-to-life effort which would have been the easy thing for Madness to do. The film does have some classic funny moments, but the band wanted it to be true to life and that it certainly is. It might not have been every music journalist's cup of free tea, but fans of the band couldn't have asked for more, and it left *Dance Craze* in the starting blocks. *Take It Or Leave It* wasn't a big success at the cinemas either though, but limited distribution was a big factor here.

Meanwhile, April 17th had seen the release of *Grey Day*, an Invaders song of old. It was backed by *Memories*, and in now predictable fashion, the single bowled itself straight into the charts and into the number four spot. It was also available in cassingle format with no extra tracks, and as a 12" single, with the added bonus of a Spanish version of *One Step Beyond* sung by Chas. Madness had heard that a Spanish band were all set to record the Prince Buster number and so decided to beat them to it with *Un Paso Adelante*. By now, Chas was pulling his weight musically and had even picked up the trumpet to add muscle to the band's brass sound.

Next stop was the epic Absolutely Madness One Step Beyond Far East Tour which was to bring a touch of Madness to Japan, New Zealand and Australia. In Japan, the band were greeted with near hysteria. Only in the land of the rising sun could

43

you buy 2 Tone cigarettes, and there were even comic books on sale showing Madness and The Specials fighting it out martial art style. Despite a hectic schedule, Madness managed to find the time to shoot a TV commercial for Honda City cars.

Life on the road Down Under was a breeze in comparison. The only problem was Lee nearly drowning when a freak wave caught him unawares while swimming off Bondi Beach. Luckily, he was saved by a couple of lifeguards who, it is said, were more interested in getting his autograph than rescuing the poor bloke.

On the way home, the band decided to play a handful of dates in the United States. All five sold out and saw the likes of David Bowie, The Jam and Pete Townsend turning up in the audience. One reason for stopping off was to get a new record deal after Sire had dropped the band following the poor showing of *Absolutely* over there. Madness were happy to see Sire go, but were sorry that *Absolutely* had been wasted on them.

The only other cloud on the horizon was The Centre For Contemporary Studies dragging up the old ghost about neo-Nazis recruiting at Madness gigs. The band did all they could to stop them selling *Bulldog* and other 'papers inside gigs, but this report stemmed from the fact that the NF and BM had been touting for business outside the Hammersmith Odeon gigs last Christmas. Again a press statement had to be issued, stating that Madness "wish to make it perfectly clear that they did not support any racist policies and hope that their fans of all ages and all nationalities do likewise."

Back in the real world, September 11th saw the release of *Shut Up* b/w *A Town With No Name* as a taster for the forthcoming *7* album. The sleeve was designed by Birmingham skinhead Paul Clewley following a competition run by the Madness fan club, but the funny thing about *Shut Up* was that those words don't appear in the song at all. When Suggs first wrote the song it was a lot longer and the words were there, but by the time it had been crafted into a three minute gem, the words had disappeared. Sentimental to the last, the band kept the original title and so *Shut Up* it was. The single was in the charts a week or so later and took up its residency in the Top Ten at the number seven spot. By now the chart compilers must have been reserving spaces for Madness singles.

On to October 2nd and the release of *7*. In lots of ways this album saw the band coming of age, or at least getting credit for being serious musicians and not just nutty characters who filled the glossy pages of the pop weeklies. Both musically and emotionally the band had done a lot of growing up over the last two years and this was reflected in the general feel of the album. The fact that it was recorded in the tropical climbs of Nassau and The Bahamas might have had a little to do with its laid back mood, but it was also clear that their frantic dance crazed days were over too. The music press loved it and it got rave reviews across the board. "Music hall spivs of the Eighties" trumpeted *Sounds* when giving it the five star treatment.

Even the band were surprised by the favourable reaction the album received and were no doubt equally pleased to see it motor up the charts to the number five spot. It was certainly better than

"America wasn't as good as Japan and Australia, but mind you, you could have a laugh there. They didn't know what bollocks meant so we always got the girl at the hotel or airport to put out a call for Mr. Harry Bollocks to come to reception. With the accent it sounded like Mr. Hairy Bollocks and we'd be on the floor with laughter."

Chrissy Boy

the occasionally patchy *Absolutely*, but whether it really did herald a new direction for the band was a little more debatable.

The lunatic tag was as much the band's fault as anybody else's. They had called their music "the nutty sound" and of course everyone expected them to always be doing whacky things. One of the reasons the band had put a label on their own sound was to prevent anyone else trying to put them in a pigeonhole marked ska or rock or what-have-you, but it completely backfired because the media just put them in the box marked madcap.

"When we described our music as the nutty sound we were just putting our own label on the sound. But I think it screwed us up in the long run, locked us into our own little jail."
Woody

The thing was Madness had never really been about throw away pop songs anyway. They had the image of being as mad as hatters, partly because they were always asked to act the fool by the media. And out of seven people, you could always count on one or two band members to come up with the goods in the fooling around department. Plus out of any photo session you could bet your last pound coin that the picture editor would choose the wackiest one possible.

(Stiff)

"We didn't make a conscious effort to be more serious. 7 is very natural, but I'm glad it was a bit less nutty and more musical."
Suggs

What's more, humour was a very big part of what the band were about, be it the slap stick variety or the more gentle, subtle kind. But while the cheeky chappies with the red noses featured in *Look In* and *My Guy* might have been the more obvious face of Madness, there was also a street-wise side that had grown up in razor blade alley, that led every day lives, that enjoyed a few pints of

45

beer of an evening, and that knew all too well that entertainment didn't have to be a million miles away from reality.

And all this was going on years before 7 came along with the recognition of the band's serious side. *Razor Blade Alley, Grey Day, Mummy's Boy* and *My Girl* could hardly be described as fodder for teenyboppers, and demonstrate a remarkable accuracy for capturing every day occurrences in three minute musical capsules. The dash of humour only went to show that if you didn't laugh at life then you had to cry. Unlike most pop bands, there was real substance behind the smiles for the camera, and maybe there lies one of Madness' greatest qualities.

The two faces of Madness were most clearly reflected in their fans. On one hand there were the younger fans who saw them purely as a nutty pop band, and who covered their bedroom walls in Madness posters. And on the other, you had the older kids, who saw people like themselves up on stage producing music that was relevant to their lives. You might get the old hand saying that the band had moved away from their roots, especially when stuff like *Driving In My Car* came out, but it was never a problem to admit that you liked Madness. And such acceptance across the board was another major factor in the band's success.

1981 was to end with a 36 date UK tour with tattoos and tights outfit The Belle Stars, and yet another hit single. The Seven Tour began its long haul around the country at Bradford's St. George's Hall on October 8th and ended with three nights at the London Dominion and a fourth London date at the Hammersmith Palais on December 19th. Despite the heavy schedule, Madness still took time out to play two Rainbow gigs with The Beat at the end of November for the Jobs For Youth Campaign.

Below: Holding the Madness 7 pose (see page 4) was not easy for photo after photo. Madness weren't slow at letting the photographer know what they thought about doing it one more time. (Stiff/Teldec)

46

For the December dates in Scotland, the band wore kilts and frightened the hell out of everyone by tossing a massive caber into the audience (for foreign readers not in the know, a caber is a giant phallic symbol native to Scotland). Nobody died because it was made of polystyrene, but eight people gave birth to kittens just before it hit them.

In amongst all the mayhem, Stiff managed to release Madness' stab at a Christmas number one with a cover version of Labbi Siffre's 1971 hit, *It Must Be Love*. It made its way into the charts the following week and ended up at number four. The video featured Chrissy Boy playing an electric guitar underwater and when it was shown on *Top Of The Pops*, presenter Jimmy Saville told the viewers not to try it at home. That must have saved a few lives that night. Still, that's the BBC for you, all heart.

It looked like Madness would finish the year as they had started it. A string of hit singles and another successful tour under their belt, but on December 22nd disaster struck for virtually every female fan of the band. Suggs got married to Ann, better known as Bette Bright. Until then, the fan club had been flooded with letters asking if the big man was spoken for, and you could almost hear the hearts breaking as news of the knot-tying reached the pop pages. Sometimes you've got to be cruel to be kind, but the cynical timing of the wedding just before Christmas should have been a matter for the House Of Commons. Suggs can just count his lucky stars that it was closed at the time to give Members Of Parliament a well-deserved holiday.

"Madness, as a group, are probably the least inclined towards superstardom of any band I've worked with. Their attitude hasn't changed particularly from when they had nothing to now, when they've got a bit of money and fame. I find that pretty unusual."

Dave Robinson

HOUSE OF FUN

1982 wasn't without its heartache either. In January, Chas had to rescue his brother from a five month stint in the Foreign Legion, which involved the Smyth family smuggling Brendan across the French border into Italy in the back of a camper van and then home to London.

The band then busied themselves with TV appearances in Europe, Japan and the States, and by going to Hollywood to make more commercials for Honda. No heartache there, but more was quite literally around the corner with the release of *Cardiac Arrest* on February 5th. The flip side was *In The City*, a song knocked out in ten minutes flat for the Honda TV commercial when the song suggested by the company turned out to be, er, clap.

Cardiac Arrest was written by Chris and Chas, after Chas had seen a man have a heart attack on the tube. The video for it was shot on an open deck double decker bus, with Lee doing his bit for sales by shouting out to bemused pedestrians, "Support London Police! Don't buy it - steal it!". The single's message was health is more important than work and it looked like being a massive hit. When it made the charts a fortnight after release it was the highest new entry, and the following week it was the highest climber. But in the end it only made it to number 14, depriving Madness of ten Top Tens in a row. The reason for its sudden lack of progress was because of Radio One's farcical decision to blank it following two deaths in DJs families. Thousands of people die every day, and it doesn't stop the BBC making comedy shows about undertakers or the like, but the world and his dog are expected to stop for Radio One Jocks.

Still, nothing could stop the nutty boys' relentless drive towards the number one spot and at the end of April they were to release both a chart-topping album and single. *Complete Madness* was released on 23rd of April and went straight in at number two. It had actually gone gold on advance sales. Within a month the album had knocked Paul McCartney off the top spot, and it even made it back there after Roxy Music had the cheek to depose it for a week. This greatest hits package included all the chart hits from *The Prince* onwards, as well as a few choice album tracks to make up the numbers. 16 slices of classic Madness including *House Of Fun* which was to be the new single released on April 30th.

It was given the big push by Stiff, coming out on 7", 12" and picture disc, all with just the one track, *Don't Look Back*, in attendance. Although the song was about the trials and tribulations of walking into a shop and buying a pack of three, there was only one place to film a video for a song with a title like that. A fun fair. As luck would have it, Lee's parents now lived in Great Yarmouth and were friendly with the local fairground owner. The season still hadn't started, so Madness were given a free run of the park to make a video. Once again, low budget was the order of the day and only one camera was used to shoot the fairground ride. In fact it

"Dave Robinson went with us on the Loop The Loop in Great Yarmouth for the House Of Fun video and all his money fell out of his pockets and his wallet fell out. He lost every bean on him!"

Woody

Above: Lee and Chas keep the engine running for the *Driving In My Car* video (Stiff)

probably cost the band more when all the money fell out of pockets when they looped the loop. The single went straight into the charts at number eight and was number one by the end of May, with ads in the music press saying, "About time too."

On the 29th of May, Madness had the notable distinction of being at the top of both the album and singles chart. They were in Japan at the time, and celebrated with nothing more than a slice of melon each. Despite being totally knackered after a long flight, they smiled and waved to fans back home via a live link up on *Top Of The Pops*. *Complete Madness* was also released on video, featuring all the videos for the singles and the Japanese TV commercials for the sum of £19.50 - a bargain at the time. And it also topped the music video charts, giving Madness the record industry's equivalent of rugby's Triple Crown.

Then on July 16th, *Driving In My Car* was released with *Animal Farm* on the B side. This time it came out in plain old 7", 7" with fold out poster, 12", and picture disc, but despite the multiple sales it was never destined to top the charts. It was catchy enough, annoyingly so in fact, but was the worst single the band ever released. It was supposed to be a piss-take of Cortina drivers and the furry dice brigade, as well as a tribute to Morris Minor vans, but never really came off. Umpteen silly noises do not a classic tune make. The 12" saw Lee take over vocal duty for a cycling version of *Driving In My Car*, entitled *Riding On My Bike.* At least the band did the right thing in the video by refusing to give The Fun Boy Three a lift, and the single still made it to the number four spot.

That month they played one of their few U.K. dates that year. It was a charity bash in aid of The Prince's Trust, and as with most of these occasions you had to be rich or well connected to get a ticket. When Prince Charles entered the royal box, compere Kid Jensen asked everyone to be upstanding for the national anthem. Then in trooped Madness, wearing kilts and tartan trousers, and playing *God Save The Queen* on kazoos. Even Charlie was beaming from ear to ear and that adds up to some smile. Lee did his flying act, and each member wore a hat with a letter on it so that when they took their bow, the word M-A-D-N-E-S-S was displayed. The band had actually played a secret gig the night before at the Bull & Gate in Kentish Town as something of a warm up. It was supposedly just for family and friends, but there was the inevitable black market for tickets too.

September was spent recording a new album and in October it was back to the land down under for a sell out tour of Oz. *Complete Madness* was number two in the Australian charts and that guaranteed full signs outside every gig. They played all the big cities like Sydney, Melbourne and Canberra, but the best gig of the tour was in Adelaide courtesy of the very appreciative audience. They also went on kiddies TV where a fool in a dragon's costume asked really deep questions like, "What is ska?". Within 20 seconds

51

someone had pulled the dragon's tongue out, but it didn't stop the verbal diarrhoea.

The band were back home in time for the release of *Rise And Fall* on November 5th and the single, *Our House*, a week later. It was hard to believe that the band could ever put a foot wrong, but the serious, almost depressing tone, of the new album surprised and disappointed a lot of people. Only *New Musical Express* raved about it in print, with some clown describing it as "the best Madness record . . . stuffed with marvellous new pop", but even those who accepted that Madness had a serious side to them must have wondered if the band had gone too far in that direction. *Melody Maker* seemed to sum it up when it said, "There'll be some confused little faces when the shrink wrapping gets ripped off this one."

"It's getting more serious in a childish sort of way."

Thommo

The album had an almost nostalgic feel to it as it yearned for a time long gone, be it the lost childhood of *Our House* and *Primrose Hill*, or the demise of once great cities in the title track. The band had high hopes for the album and no doubt expected a few slaps on the back for their progression, but few shared their belief in the LP. Only the opening tracks on both sides had any real life to them, but as Lee said, you can't keep writing *Benny Bullfrog* when you see what's happening around you - hence *Blue-Skinned Beast,* a dig at the tabloids for the way they had hung on Thatcher's every word during the Falklands War.   At least the band were taking on serious subjects close to their heart, and hats off to the boys for doing so, but it was just too heavy for most people.

The album had already gone gold before its release so its success was assured, but it never went higher than the number ten spot. Most kids who got a Madness album in their bulging stocking that Christmas probably got *Complete Madness*, with *Rise And Fall*

Below: Madness getting the Maddiemobile ready for the road and (opposite page) out and about in it. The video for *Driving In My Car* showed a Morris Minor being dropped from a height and falling apart as it hit the ground. This was an old banger and not the much cherished Maddiemobile you'll be glad to hear. (Stiff)

losing its way in the pre-Christmas avalanche of releases.

Happy go lucky singles were the public face of Madness, with few bothering to listen to the words and their message. *Embarrassment* was actually about a family's reaction to a girl having a half-caste baby, but few would have guessed after hearing it a few times on the radio. Albums though are a different species all together. You have more time to listen to them and take in the

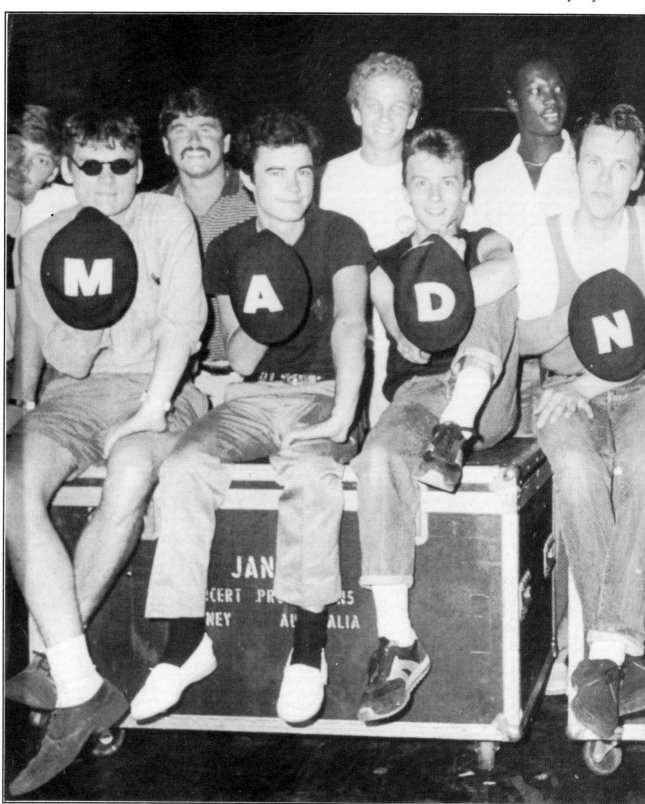

54

lyrics, and with *Rise And Fall* you were being invited into the private world of Madness and maybe that clown at *NME* understood that more than most.

With *Our House*, you were on more familiar ground. A musical jolly beano that was more like the band that watched *Snow White And The Seven Dwarves* on their tour bus, and who wreaked havoc one night in Zürich when they were given a Swiss army knife

Below: Madness met the England cricket team when in Australia. On the far right is Madness sound man, Ian "Dad" Horne who is now "Grandad" (Stiff)

each. They spent the whole night walking around their hotel unscrewing everything in sight then putting it back on - upside down. Door handles, door numbers, the works.

Our House was accompanied by *Walking With Mr. Wheeze* and the cover was done by Karen Allen, a six year old pupil at Camden Town Infants School. It made it to number five, and thereby secured Madness' crown as single artists of the year for the third year in a row. In 1982 alone, the band had sold over 1.35 million singles.

At the end of the year they toured Holland, Belgium and Germany, complete with wives, girlfriends, and babies, but it had been well over a year since they had toured Britain. The situation was remedied in February 1983 with a fourteen date tour billed as "The Greatest Show On Earth", starting with two nights at Newcastle Town Hall on the 21st and 22nd, and finishing at Edinburgh Playhouse on March 9th.

Just to make sure everyone remembered who Madness were, Stiff released the double A side *Tomorrow's Just Another Day* and *Madness Is All In The Mind* on February 11th. It was trotted out in the by now familiar picture disc and 12" formats as well as the 7", and continued the band's domination of the Top Ten by making it to the number eight spot. The 12" was a bit special, with Elvis Costello providing vocals on a re-recorded version of *Tomorrow's Just Another Day*. Old Suggs was obviously having an easy time of it

Below: Never work with animals. The doves used for this photo session were tied to band member's with wire, but it didn't stop them trying to fly away or crapping over everybody's shoes (Stiff)

56

"When you start out it's really different because you're doing everything yourself and know exactly what's going on. When people start doing things for you it spoils it quite a lot. You don't have to lose control, but it happens because there's so much work, you have to rely on other people. There's too much going on - it's got too big now."

Barso

because it is Carl singing on *Madness Is All In The Mind* too.

The tour entourage once again included families and pets, while the support slot went to Jo Boxers whose big hit, *Boxer Beat*, entered the charts the same week as *Tomorrow's Just Another Day*. It was the Boxers' first major tour and this time it was the new boys making all the noise and living it up. Chas, Suggs and Lee would sometimes join the road crew for late night drinking sessions, but the novelty of hitting the road had worn off ages ago for these old hands.

Elvis Costello joined Madness on stage at the London shows to sing his version of *Tomorrow's Just Another Day*, and on all dates Madness were complemented by a classical string quartet and Dick Cuthell's cornet. The tour was the success you'd imagine, but in some ways it was too successful.

Some of the venues were bigger than would have been liked, and although that let more people in to see the band, those at the back might as well have been watching on TV. After gigs, the band also found that their coach was being mobbed by fans and it wasn't something they were comfortable with. It was too Duran Duran, and Madness never wanted to be part of the stars on a pedestal rock circus.

On the tour, Barso had become more distant from the others. Nothing major, but it was obvious that his family life was assuming greater importance to him. At the end of March, the band were booked to appear on German TV, but Mike didn't show up. A wardrobe assistant stood in for him, and nobody seemed any the wiser, but it was the first time a member of the band had let the others down like that. Later, the episode was played down, with the

57

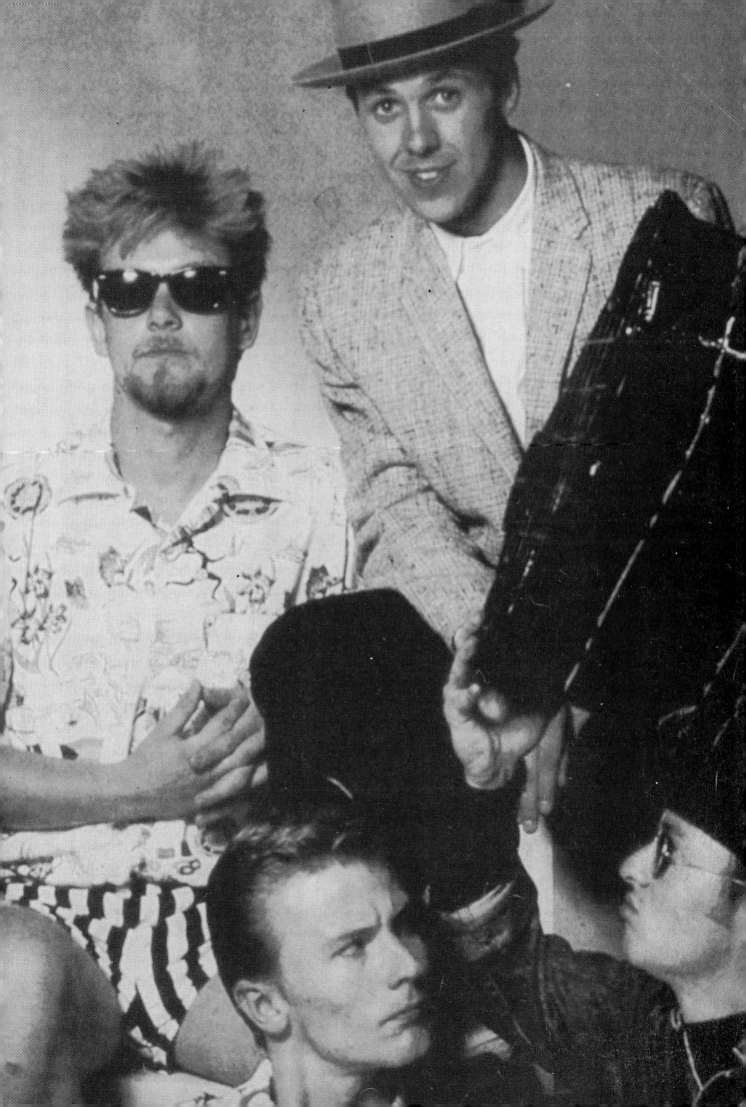

others saying they knew he would miss it because he was moving house, but at the same time seeds were being sown for Mike Barson's eventual departure.

Better news arrived in April with Madness signing to Geffen in the United States. Despite three previous visits, Madness had hardly made any impact out there, and this new deal gave them a chance to put things right. An album entitled *Madness* was released, containing most of their hits plus a few tracks off *Rise And Fall*, and *Our House* was put out as a single. This time there was a lot more radio interest and the band's videos were ideal for MTV, the TV station dedicated to music. And the result? *Our House* at number seven in the U.S. charts that July. Now, all that was needed was for Stiff to pull their finger out in Europe, where their constant changing of distributors meant no momentum was being built up despite a lot of success, and all would have been rose bushes and tulips in the Madness garden.

Above: Ex-Specials, The Fun Boy Three turned up in the *Driving In My Car* video, hitching a lift to Coventry. Fortunately, Madness didn't pick them up (Stiff)

That August Madness headed for the States where they played 25 dates in five weeks. Some of the shows saw them support The Police and David Bowie in front of massive crowds, but they also headlined smaller gigs in front of two to five thousand people a night. It was the best organised tour to date, despite some fool issuing a writ while the band were in New York for money owed for allegedly setting up the Geffen deal.

Back in England, things were pretty quiet. The band did play a benefit for the Sizewell B Campaign at the Victoria Apollo in April, which saw them jamming together with UB40 for *One In Ten* and

Madness. And in May they had headlined the CND rally at Brockwell Park, saving the day after The Damned, Hazel O'Connor and The Style Council had failed to impress the crowd of 10,000. At least Madness weren't interested in preaching. There was no patronising bollocks, just 200 t-shirts thrown into the crowd, take them or leave them.

Later that month they recorded *Wings Of A Dove*, and then everyone headed off for a well-earned holiday. Barso decided to tour Europe in a Dormobile van, and for weeks on end the others heard nothing from him. Stiff even had to 'phone up his mum to find out where he was because he contacted her the most. He only arrived back in London a day before filming started on the video for *Wings Of A Dove* which didn't exactly make him everybody's favourite person of the month.

The single was released on August 12th, with the Madness sound being beefed up by the Creighton Steel Sounds, a steel band from Muswell Hill, and The First Born Inspirational Church Of The Living God gospel choir. Carl had first seen the gospel choir on the Channel 4 art show, *Black On Black*, which was hosted by none other than Pauline Black of The Selecter fame, and it was his idea to ask them to sing on the single. At first the choir weren't too keen to appear on a pop song, but did so in the end because of the message of peace it would carry and thanks to a lot of arm twisting by Carl.

It was released with *Behind The 8 Ball* on the flip side, and once again, Paul Clewley designed the sleeve. The single went right up the charts to the number two spot, with UB40's first number one, *Red Red Wine,* preventing Madness from getting to the top.

By then, the finishing touches had been put on Madness' own Liquidator studios, work had started on another album, and the future for the band was looking very bright. There was even talk of a

"If it makes a few people think about it, it's worth it."

Bedders

(Stiff/David Corio)

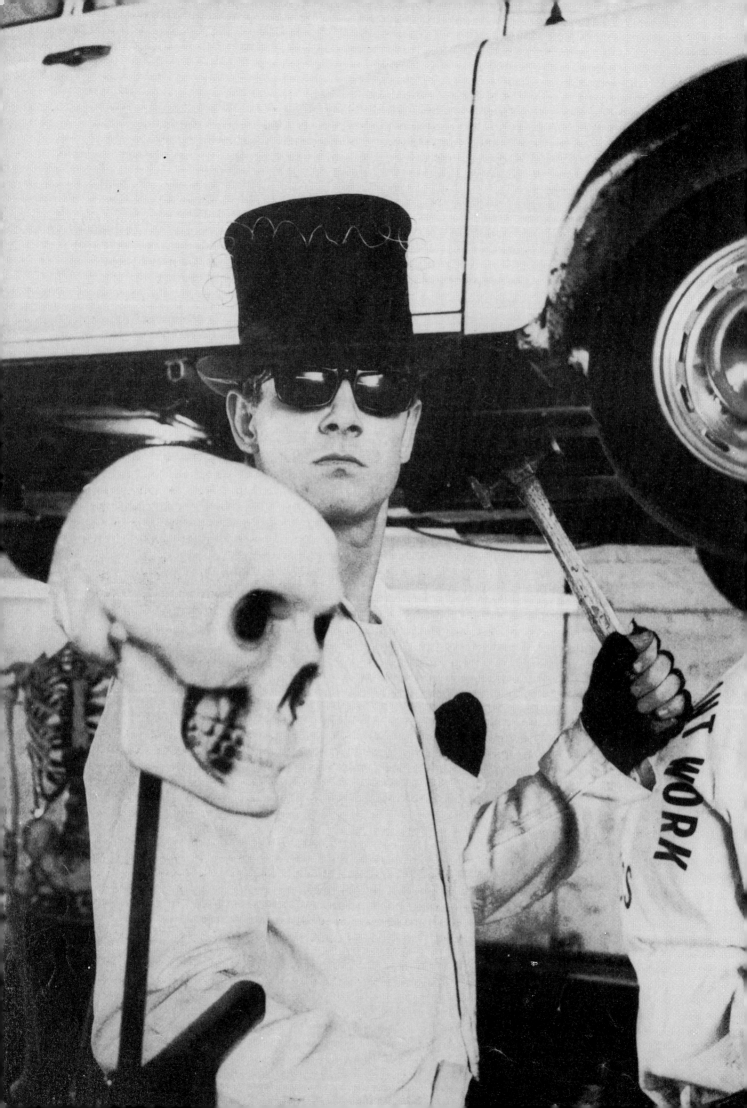

Madness TV show, which was to see Madness being swept to power following a crisis General Election. But if these wise men were going to run the country, it would have been without Mike Barson. On October 4th, a day before Lee's birthday, Mike announced that he would be leaving the band after the album had been recorded. Lee and Chris had been expecting it because Mike was spending more and more time in Holland with his wife and he had grown to hate touring. But even so, the announcement came as a shock on the day. There was a minute of silence then Lee shouted, "Okay lads, let's get the bastard!".

Later that month, on the 28th, *The Sun And The Rain* was released, but Mike had disappeared on the eve of its release to tour Yugoslavia. The video for the single required rain and even that didn't happen. Typical British weather. Rains all year and then the day you want it to, it doesn't. So the band hired an old fire engine to do the trick. Then to cap it all a Chinese restaurant owner 'phoned the police when Lee started messing about with a rocket tied to his back.

The single had *Fireball XL5* as a B side on the 7" (hence Lee and the rocket on his back), and the 12" had the added attraction of a live version of *My Girl* which had been recorded at the Brighton Conference Centre during the last tour. It was to be the band's third Top Ten hit of the year, peaking at number five.

On December 21st, the Madness Xmas Party at the Lyceum in aid of Greenpeace was to be Mike Barson's farewell gig. Madness were never political, but they did give their support to Greenpeace and CND because at least these organisations got off their arses and tried to do something positive for the world. On the night, Camden Town's Bonsai Forest opened proceedings (their debut single, *The Great Escape*, had been produced by Bedders), and were followed by Ian Dury & The Music Students. Then Neil from TV's *The Young Ones* came on, but try though he did, the terrace chants of "Madness!" meant only the best would do.

Madness turned in a great set lasting 90 minutes and were joined for *Razor Blade Alley* by a very capable blow-up doll. At the end of the night, confetti, balloons and Monopoly money showered the crowd, and everyone went home happier and richer. Afterwards, there was a bash organised at a Covent Garden youth club which Chris and Bedders had trouble getting into because they had no tickets! Suggs didn't make it either because he was off on a skiing holiday, but more importantly, Mike Barson's face was missing too. Something the band would have to start getting used to.

"Mike Barson has decided to retire from Madness and the wonderful world of pop music and is settling permanently in Amsterdam. The mild-mannered foundation stone will be sorely missed by Madness with sadness".

So read the press release announcing Mike's departure. Without Mike, things would never be the same. For one, the casting vote had gone. With seven, it was hands up and the majority carried the day, but that wasn't the case with just six and there were

Above: Madness relaxing in *Our House* (Stiff)

no plans to find a replacement. In fact the remaining Maddy Boys were all frantically trying to learn the piano themselves!

Mike had also started the band and had held it together during the first two or three years when it looked like the band were going nowhere. Slowly. And although, the song-writing was now being done by all members of the band (thanks partly to the home recording equipment Dave Robinson had given each band member), it was Mike who had at least part credit for penning most of the band's hits to date.

He would indeed be missed by one and all, but it was plain to see that he had decided that his family life in Holland now meant more to him than touring the world with a pop band. Priorities change as you get older - it's a fact of life. There was no question of the rest quitting the band though. They would fight the good fight without him for the time being. And if nothing else, Barso's departure kept everyone on their toes, and in some ways brought the rest of the band closer together for what were to be testing times ahead.

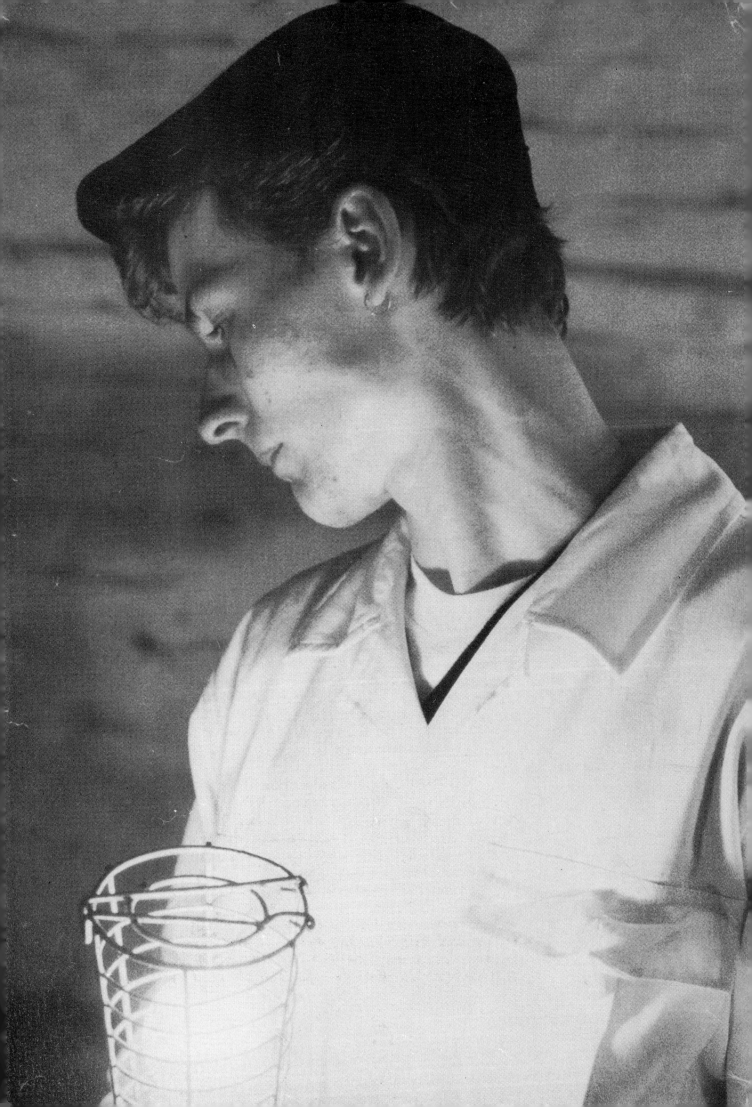

KEEP MOVING

IT was business as usual for Madness at the start of 1984. January saw the band in Poland to appear on TV shows, but they were paid in the local currency and couldn't take it out of the country. So after buying as many East German electric goods as they could carry, and as much Russian vodka as they could drink, they gave the change away and headed home.

Mike Barson might have left the band, but he lived on in vinyl. On January 30th, *Michael Caine* was released with *If You Think There's Something* on the B side. The actor Michael Caine actually did the voice over for the single because his daughter was a big Madness fan, but he went back to the States before the video was shot. Not that the record was about him anyway. The troubles of Northern Ireland provided the inspiration, but as the man himself would say, not a lot of people know that. The single made its way into the charts and settled at the number 11 spot.

While everyone and his dog waited for the release of the new album, the band kept themselves busy with guest appearances at a kiddies' Valentine disco, and Lee and Chas joined old mucker John Hasler in The Skiff Skats for a couple of gigs. *Keep Moving* eventually came out on February 20th. The Madness name guaranteed it would sell, and it made it to the number six spot, but it was quite a disappointing album all in. Dreary was a word not often associated with Madness, but it did sum up the album quite nicely. Much of it had been completed without Barso, but the indifference of the others was starting to shine through and the only moving being done seemed to be of the going through the motions variety.

One Better Day was perhaps the only track on the album beside *Michael Caine* that deserved the single treatment and it was duly released on May 12th, with the band just back from another American tour. The B side was *Guns*, which was recorded in the band's new Liquidator studios, and Stiff pulled out all the stops with this one. 7", picture disc, 7" with poster sleeve and a 12" with the bonus track, *Sarah*. It made the Top 20, sliding in at number 17, but was to prove the least successful single the band had released to date.

The band had other problems too thanks to the increasingly soured relationship between them and Stiff. Madness were the label's biggest earners, but over the years they had become just another "viable product", and they didn't make music anymore, they "shifted units". That situation was only likely to get worse now that Stiff had merged with Island.

Before, Stiff was run from a house and you could call in and count on Dave Robinson to make a snap decision about anything and everything. But after the merger, Stiff became just a small part of the Island empire, tucked away in a few offices in a far larger building. And although the office furniture was more impressive, the Stiff supremo didn't wield the instant power he once did.

"We just write the songs and they go on the LP, and that's all."
Chrissy Boy

Left: Woody (Stiff)

Above: The release of *Michael Caine* coincided with an outbreak of wearing Michael Caine glasses.

So when the Stiff contract ended on 21st of May, the band decided not to sign on the dotted line again. Of course, there were other reasons for leaving Stiff. It was a label of mottoes and one of them was "a tired band is a happy band". That basically meant keep the band on the road so that the records get promoted and the money keeps rolling in. I don't know about the happy bit, but it must have put a smile on the face of Stiff's accountant.

Right from the off, Madness had dreamed of earning enough money to build their own studio and start their own label, and leaving Stiff would give them the opportunity to finally control their own destiny. They had tried to do that with Stiff, and at least were no longer on the road every week of the year, but still things were happening without them agreeing to it. The British Beef commercial that Dave Robinson wrote and directed was a good example. It was an obvious rip-off of Madness which the band knew nothing about until it was made, and wanted nothing to do with, not least because two of them, Mike and Woody, were veggies.

All of the above obviously contributed to Madness' decision to leave Stiff and strike out alone, but although it's rarely said, the straw that broke the camel's back must have been Stiff's decision to release the Tracey Ullman version of *My Girl* under the name of *My Guy*. Of course the band made pleasant noises about it, Bedders even played on it and you're always going to get a kick out of one of your songs being covered. But the bottom line was that a great song was completely ruined in less than three minutes flat. It must have taken some doing, but our Tracey managed it with amazing ease.

There was talk of Madness having to change their name or even split, but there was no need for either. The contract had expired and Madness were free agents. It was like a huge weight off their shoulders, and that summer Madness started bubbling again. They had their own studio and office and were looking to use it as a base for themselves plus a handful of other bands.

By August, Madness were ready to announce the formation of their own record label. It was originally going to be called Nutty Sounds, but eventually they decided to plump for Zarjazz. The name came from the sci-fi comic, *2000AD* and meant brilliant or great in the alien tongue of Betelguese. A manufacturing and distribution deal was struck with Earth-dwellers, Virgin, so freeing the band to get on with what they did best, making music.

Now all that had to be done was releasing the first Zarjazz record. The year before, when Madness were on *Top Of The Pops* to perform *The Sun And The Rain*, they had bumped into Feargal Sharkey of The Undertones fame. He was working on a variety of projects, including a band called The Assembly who were also on the show to perform their hit, *Never Never*.

Carl had written a song called *Listen To Your Father* which the band just couldn't get right, so a few days after the TV show they gave old Feargal a bell to see if he would like to come down and see what he thought of it. He ended up doing the vocals and the song was recorded in March, 1984. Seven months later, on October 1st, *Listen To Your Father* by Feargal Sharkey became the first release on the Zarjazz label and did everyone proud by reaching number 23.

The next release was by Suggs and Carl under the guise of The Fink Brothers. The name was borrowed from the bad guy

"The main thing for me is that if you see a Zarjazz record you know it'll be a good record with a good B side and it'll be well done."

Chas

Below: Madness keep moving (Stiff)

69

mutants, Fink and Mean, who were the sworn enemies of Judge Dredd in *2000AD*. Anyone would have thought the boys had shares in the comic the way they promoted it. The single was electro-hip hop, as heard by the Fink Brothers in the New York clubs, and was called *Mutants In Mega-City One*. It was released on January 28th, but despite a lot of press coverage, and its appearance in various formats including a square picture disc, it only made it to number 50 in the charts.

A number of bands were being linked to Zarjazz, including Charm School, Tom Morley of Scritti Politti and Liverpool's The Farm. Madness had also wanted to release something by the gospel choir who had appeared on *Wings Of A Dove*, but Stiff had signed them while Madness were in the States the last time. Good though some of them were, all had to take a back seat while work took place on *Starvation*, a charity single put together by Madness and friends.

"We bought the Madness office in our heyday with Stiff so that if anything happened we had our own place. Once we'd built the studio downstairs, it seemed a bit of a waste of all the people here. We decided we could run at least five or six bands from here with all the facilities we've got."

Chas

Above: Although no longer with the band, Barso appeared on the last two Stiff singles, *Michael Caine* and *One Better Day*. *Victoria Gardens* would probably have been released as a single too if Madness had stayed with Stiff (Virgin)

The project was started in December, 1984, after a Madness fan, Mick Tuohy, had walked into the Liquidator studios and suggested that Madness record the old Pioneers' classic, *Starvation*, in aid of the Ethiopian famine appeal. Madness thought it would be

Right: Chrissy Boy (Stiff)

70

a good idea to involve others and gave Jerry Dammers a ring. Before they knew it, Liquidator was full to the brim with members of UB40, The Specials, General Public and The Pioneers to name just a few. The final result was described by Pioneer Jackie Robinson as "better than the original", but by the time it was released on February 25th, the project had been totally dwarfed by Band Aid and the *Do They Know It's Christmas?* hit.

Band Aid of course topped the charts and as well as raising a fortune for famine relief, it also resurrected a lot of flagging careers. Meanwhile, UB40 had donated their entire £100,000 profits from their African tour to help ease the suffering, and did so with zero publicity. *Starvation* eventually charted at number 33 and would have gone a lot higher if it had been afforded the radio play it deserved.

The main purpose of Zarjazz though was for the release of Madness material and it wasn't until a year after the label's birth that *Yesterday's Men* was released on August 23rd. The title didn't refer to the comeback of Madness, as some may have thought, but to the silver spoon brigade and the out to lunch politicians who rule the country despite having long since passed their sell-by date. It was to be Zarjazz's first Top 20 hit, but failed to capture the band's former glory with its high of 18. Good to see 2 Tone supremo, Jerry Dammers, popping up on keyboards though, and in many ways it was one of the best songs Madness ever did. Hats off to Suggs and Chrissy Boy who shared the writing credit.

The real problem now was that Virgin were giving the band too much freedom. At the start of a year they were given a large sum of money to do what they liked with and left to get on with it. At Stiff, they had been taken in hand and were always being given things to do. The heavy workload at Stiff had become a real problem, but now the total lack of direction was becoming just as bad. Getting help was no easy task either because the band were working with people in big offices who, try though they did, just didn't understand them the way Dave Robinson and Stiff had.

They did manage to get a new album together though, which was called *Mad Not Mad* (and not *Lost In The Museum* as had been predicted on the run-in groove of *Yesterday's Men*), and was released on September 30th. It made it to number 19 and Madness were happy enough with the finished article, but there was now a feeling of indifference if not unhappiness towards band life. Writing without Barso had proved more difficult than they thought it would, not least because they were rejecting anything with a ska or reggae feel in case they were accused of trotting out the same old formula. Perhaps the band were trying too hard to shake off their old nutty image too. Whatever, such barriers didn't help matters and all of a sudden Madness became more of a chore than the fun it had been for so long.

"My attitude to success is that it's a joke. It's all in your own imagination or ego."

Woody

The cost of the album had also eaten up most of their funds. The wad that Virgin had given them was also meant to pay all of the band's other overheads including the wages bill. 13 people were on the payroll, and even when Madness weren't touring, they kept paying the road crew because they were their mates. What's more, bands were getting free studio time at Liquidator, which earned

Right: Lee (Stiff)

Madness a lot of praise, but little else, and at the end of the day somebody had to pay the bills.   It soon left the band in a lot of financial debt to their label, and the strain   only added to the problems within the band.   It also meant that as time went on, Virgin were increasingly paying the pipers and calling the tune.

On October 19th, *Uncle Sam* backed by *Please Don't Go* was released.   It was the most upbeat single since *Wings Of A Dove*, but the fickleness of the record buyer only saw it to the number 21 spot. It was the first time in 21 singles that Madness had not made the Top 20. Not that any chart placing wasn't good, but it did underline Madness' gradual decline that now seemed irreversible.   A new generation of kids had come along and obviously had better things to spend their money on - including the American commercialisation of British life *Uncle Sam* spoke out against.

Dance music is always best heard live and that's where Madness were always going to be on top form.   A Mad Not Mad Tour was organised to get them back on the road, starting in Cork,

(Stiff)

Southern Ireland, on 23rd of October. By the 30th, the tour had reached the British mainland, with new 2 Tone signings, The Friday Club, in the support slot. Madness gave the fans what they wanted to hear, dropping the likes of *Driving In My Car* and *Cardiac Arrest* for the never failing charms of *One Step Beyond* and *Night Boat To Cairo*, and a new face, Seamus Beaghan, played piano for the band. The tour ended with two nights at the Hammersmith Odeon on 23rd and 24th of November, and although nobody knew it at the time, it was to be their last major tour. Bar any comebacks of course.

The year ended with the band playing a Christmas Party For The Unemployed in Finsbury Park. Ian Dury joined the band on stage for a few numbers, and in the audience for the first time since leaving Madness was Mike Barson. Then on 30 December a Mad Not Mad Party was held at Hammersmith Odeon, with the set being recorded and released as a blue vinyl promo.

January 18th, 1986, saw the release of the Scritti Politti cover, *The Sweetest Girl*, with *Jenny (A Portrait Of)* on the B side. For all the true romantics, it also came as a Valentine's Day 7" double pack, with the other single offering *Tears You Can't Hide* and *Call Me*. It was an excellent version of a much underrated song and deserved to be a big hit, but number 35 was the best it could do.

(Stiff)

The Liquidator studios were taking on the shape of a military HQ with Madness plotting their next move in what was becoming a war against Virgin. Things were really that bad between band and label. Despite a string of hits to their name, Madness were suffering from a total lack of confidence in what they were doing and it showed. Tension grew between the band members as they tried to keep the good ship Madness afloat, and things became so sour that Lee spent most of his time away from the others, working on *The Nutty Boys* comic and with the 20,000 strong fan club.

With things the way they were the last thing the band needed was a long tour. So, like lemmings rushing to their death, Madness headed Down Under for four weeks of sheer hell. And just to add to the pain they called in on the USA on the way home. There, Geffen described them in a press release as, "six zany,

Above: **Madness on a desert island for** *Uncle Sam*(Stiff) Below: **The taxi ride from** *Michael Caine* (Stiff)

happy-go-lucky lads from North London", but for once nobody was interested in living up to it. The funny thing was the U.S. dates went really well, but the time for laughing had stopped.

Back home, Madness turned out for an Artists Against Apartheid gig with the superb ska outfit, The Potato 5, at Brixton Academy, and they also played the main stage at that year's Glastonbury CND Festival. But it was all over for the band bar the shouting and in early September they finally let the world in on the secret.

(Stiff)

The press handout said it all.

"After four hundred Top Ten singles, three record labels, the odd video, two managers, countless innuendoes and being banned from here to eternity for our lack of professionalism by people with as much flair as a yoghurt carton, the 'nutty' ghost train grinds to a halt, pulls into the station: terminal Madness.

"Oh what fun we had! But for now it's a heartfelt thanks to all who helped us on our way, particularly our fans and friends. We came, we saw, we left."

Madness.

The Seven Year Itch (Part One)

Virgin responded as all true record labels do. They released a farewell single in the hope of one more ride on the Madness gravy train. *(Waiting For) The Train* backed by *Maybe In Another Life* was released in every virtually every format imaginable. 7", shaped picture disc, 12" with a tacky *Seven Year Scratch* medley of

Above: Mad not mad (Virgin / Anton Corbijn)

Madness faves, and 12" with an 8 page souvenir colour booklet. All good stuff, and even Mike Barson couldn't resist jumping aboard the last train to Madness. He was back to tinkle the ivories as only the band's founder could.

The actual song was classic Madness. They had reached the end of the line in so many ways and it was a fitting last piece in the Madness jigsaw. It was released on October 27th, and if it wasn't for the usual Christmas deluge of releases it would surely have gone higher than number sixteen.

Seven years of Madness had come to an end. 23 singles, all Top Twenty hits bar two, and seven Top Twenty albums had seen to it that Madness were a household name. And now they were to be no more. A lot of the enjoyment of being in the band seemed to have disappeared and there was little point continuing as things were. At least now, they could call it a day and still be on speaking terms rather than let things deteriorate to the point where splitting was the only option.

It was a sad day for British pop music, but an even sadder one for the thousands of kids who had championed Madness since the days of *The Prince*. But there was no need for tears. The nutty train might have ground to a halt, but what a journey the band and its fans had enjoyed. And the press release was spot on. Oh what fun we had along the way!

YESTERDAY'S MEN

AFTER seven years of living, sleeping and eating Madness, what else was there to do, but reform? In fact, the band didn't really close down completely anyway. The split happened because Bedders and Woody had different ideas for the band and rather than just leave the band and Madness continue, it was decided to call it a day. But that still left Suggs, Chrissy Boy, Lee and Carl with all the time in the world to do not a lot. And more importantly, they still wanted to work together as a group.

So after a few months of thumb-twiddling, it was decided that the foursome should keep the flag flying and see what life was left in the old bones. Things would have to be different, and if they didn't want to end up playing *One Step Beyond* for the rest of their lives (great song if you catch it live once every two years, but a bit boring after the nine hundredth time of playing it) a name change was called for.

The search for a new moniker was thrown open to the listeners of Radio One, but it was never likely that anyone happy to be fed a constant diet of chart rubbish would produce anything even half-decent. Japanese radio did its best too, but nothing doing there either.

The Wasp Factory tickled a few fancies. It was the title of Ian Bank's classic first novel, a book enthusiastically read by Carl, Lee, Suggs and Chris. In an interview for *Melody Maker*, Carl mentioned that The Wasp Factory was a possible name. Then, the following week, a band wrote in saying they were already called The Wasp Factory and begged the boys to think of another name. Decisions, decisions. So many names to choose from and in the end they plump for The Madness. Other names toyed with were The Earthmen, The One, and More, so maybe The Madness wasn't that bad after all.

The financial disaster that Zarjazz had become was put to bed, the Liquidator studios were leased out and The Madness were signed directly to Virgin. All of the above solved a lot of the band's problems at a stroke, but it also meant that the people employed by Madness had to lose their jobs. It wasn't something the band enjoyed doing, but there was just no alternative.

And so to a single to herald this brave new beginning. On February 25th, 1988, *I Pronounce You* was released with *Patience* on the B side of the 7". An old Madness track, *4.B.F.* made it on to other formats, demonstrating that links with the past hadn't been cut entirely. What was a major change though was that the band were no longer using the production services of Messrs. Langer and Winstanley. *I Pronounce You* was catchy, if a little plodding, but it was never going to be a big hit and number 44 was about its mark in life. You could almost see the Madness of old struggling to make itself heard, but it just didn't come off.

"We allowed ourselves a couple of months to think about it, because it was a big thing to split after about nine years. We got so bored after two weeks that we decided to get back together."
Chas

"They must need to pay the mortgage is one's immediate reaction."
NME review of
I Pronounce You

Left: Bedders (Stiff)

The only appearance the band were to make was on Channel 4's *Friday Night Live*. The lads did a sketch with Josie Lawrence that was never going to work and didn't. Then The Madness, their ranks swollen by John Hasler on drums and Dick Cuthell on trumpet, played the single and *Beat The Bride*. Nothing to make you rush home from the pub to see, but worth setting the old video for.

Then came the album, imaginatively entitled *The Madness*. This time around the boys tried to learn from their mistakes and managed to record the whole thing for peanuts. That was until Virgin wanted a say in the mixing and sent along a producer at £1,500 a day for over a week. To beef up the sound, The Madness called on old friends like Jerry Dammers, Dick Cuthell, UB40's Earl Falconer, various Attractions and the brass section of The Potato 5.

It was released on April 23rd, but barely made any impression on the charts, spending just a week at the number 65 spot, despite its good points like *Beat The Bride* and *Nightmare Nightmare*. The fact that Virgin put little muscle behind it was partly to blame and then there was the simple fact that The Madness just didn't capture even past fan's imagination. Not totally anyway. The music press didn't go overboard about it either, but at least the new generation of journalists gave it the benefit of the doubt with Q saying that it "reveals a fresh approach from an agile four-piece willing to experiment with different songs and song structures."

The biggest mistake made by The Madness though was the choice of *What's That* as a single. That one must have been lucky to scrape on to the album. *Be Good Boy* appeared on the B side and the 12" added *Flashings*, but the only real joy was buying the two picture discs, slotting them together and having all three tracks. It received minimal radio exposure, and for the first time in Madness history, the boys failed to crack even the lowest reaches of the charts.

Things obviously weren't working out as had been hoped. The band members were pulling in different directions, trying to salvage something from the sinking ship. Suggs and Chrissy Boy wanted to experiment more with studio technology, while Carl still wanted a live band. If things had gone better with the album, the band would certainly have toured, but it was a vicious circle really. No tour meant poor album sales and poor album sales meant no tour.

The Madness just seemed to totally lack the vital spark that was Madness. The press release announcing the arrival of the band back in March had about as much life to it as a graveyard full of dodos:

"After adjustments the band are now Suggs, Lee Thompson, Chris Foreman and Carl Smyth. The band shall be known as The Madness.

"They have spent the last year writing, playing and producing an album. The album shall be known as The Madness. A single from The Madness will be out soon and the direction and the sound shall be known as The Madness.

"The Madness will be shooting visuals to accompany the album and also seeking out like minds to perform live."

Nobody would be labelling this lot nutty, that much was certain. But out with the bathwater went the baby, and the subtle humour that was always Madness at their best was nowhere to be seen. The ads for the album and single were little better. Totally faceless, almost corporate creations that signified apathy in the ranks of The Madness.

For their part, Virgin weren't too impressed with the way things were going. They hadn't even put the money up for a video for *What's That*, which the band saw as quite an insult given their track record in that department. Eventually they gave The Madness an ultimatum. Either Virgin heard some new songs within a month or they wouldn't renew the band's contract.

It was actually a blessing in disguise for the band. They owed Virgin a lot of money and were like condemned men doing

(Virgin)

83

hard labour, trying to come up with a hit single to pay some of the money back. Then along comes Virgin and they are told they can go if they don't write any more songs! Obviously Virgin still had the Madness back catalogue to make up the losses, but for Suggs especially, this was too good an escape chance to miss. He had wanted out for a while, but didn't know how he would tell the others. The day he finally plucked up the courage saw The Madness come to an end and all concerned a lot happier with life.

(Virgin)

They must have been gluttons for punishment to even risk a comeback after the trials and tribulations of the last year or so of Madness, but they'd given it their best shot and you can never ask for more than that. For Bedders and Woody things had worked out rather better however.

"We split because of health reasons. We got sick of it, but not of each other!"

Thommo

After leaving Madness, both signed up with Voice Of The Beehive, a five piece outfit put together by two American sisters, Tracey Bryn and Melissa Belland. They recorded a single on Food Records, *Just A City,* and were then snapped up by London Records. Bedders left shortly afterwards, but Woody stayed behind and found himself back in the charts. *Let It Bee*, the band's debut album released in June 1988, made it to number 13 and went gold, and to that can be added another top twenty album and a handful of entries in the single charts Of all the post-Madness bands, Voice Of The Beehive were by far the most successful.

Bedders never intended staying with Voice Of The Beehive. Of all the Maddie Boys, it was Mark who most regularly played away, turning up on releases by the likes of Strawberry Switchblade and the hauntingly superb, Shipbuilding, which was a Top Forty hit for Robert Wyatt back in '83.

84

Above: Voice Of The Beehive featuring Woody (second left) and Bedders (far right) (London)

"We're not called Butterfield 8 anymore. We're called The Butterfield 8 now."

Bedders

He was all set for a solo career, but ended up joining up with ex-Higsons' sax player, Terry Edwards, in Butterfield 8 after saying he would help him out on a few tracks. After recording a demo, the band were snapped up by Go! Discs, and in the expanded line-up was the same Seamus Beaghan who had played with Madness on the Mad Not Mad Tour. A single, *Watermelon Man*, and an album, *Blow!*, were released but chart success eluded them. Not that they were really looking for it with Herbie Hancock covers and other jazz instrumentals.

After The Madness fiasco, Suggs turned his back on music for a while, and concentrated on a TV career, doing odds and ends for Channel 4, and eventually hosting *Music Box* three nights a week on satellite TV. He also did some compere work, hosting a weekly alternative comedy show at Harlesden's Mean Fiddler. That left Carl to go off wheeling and dealing before joining Go! Discs as an A&R man, and Lee and Chris to more or less carry on where the others had left off.

They hadn't really written together during the Madness days so it was quite a change for both of them, but come the end of 1988, they had three new songs under their belt which they touted around the big name record labels. Neither of them expected to be snapped up immediately, but doing the rounds without the Madness name proved a hard slog. Labels wanted to know what the band would be called, would they be touring, what package were they offering, could Lee be a front man and so the questions continued.

Thing was, Lee and Chris didn't have many of the answers. They planned to get a deal and then take it from there. In the end they signed to Link Records, a Kent-based street label who snapped them up on the strength of a ropey demo. It was Link who also

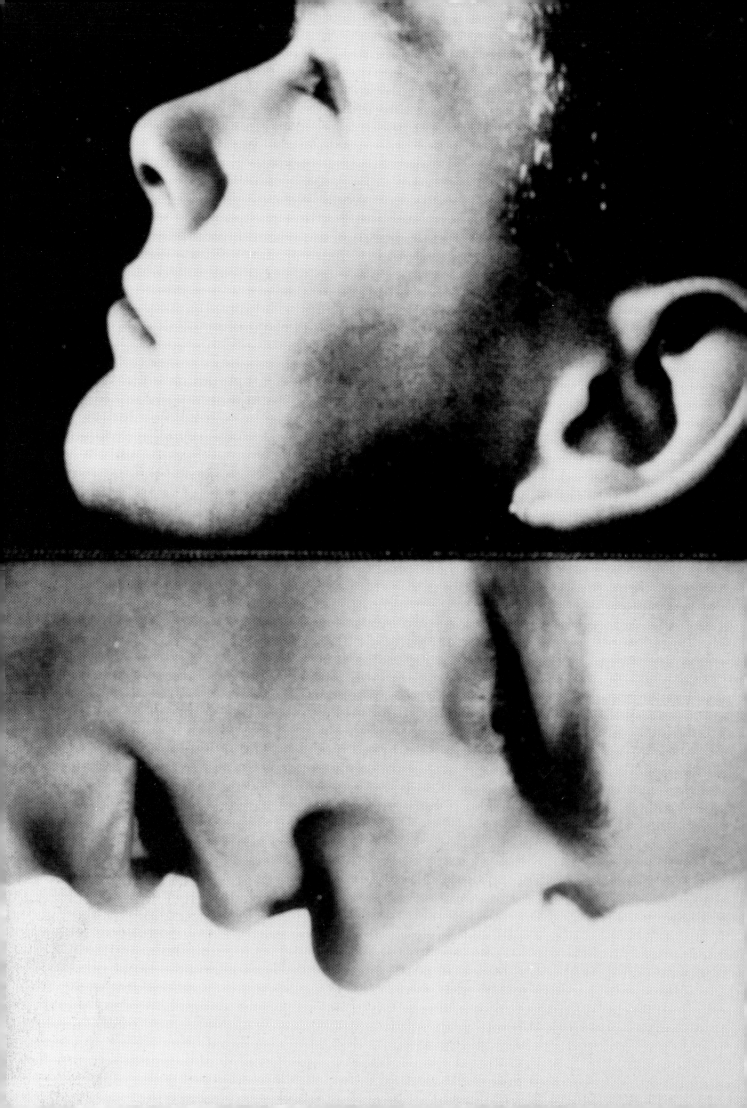

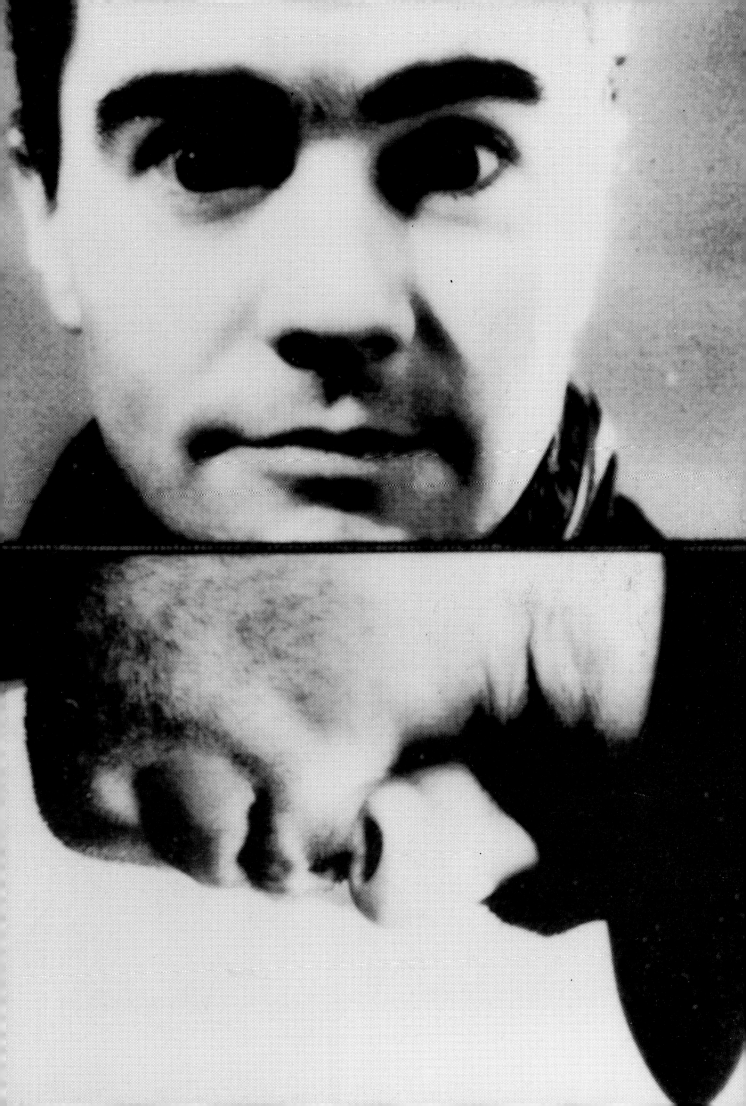

suggested a name for the twosome - The Nutty Boys - which with hindsight was a big mistake. An album, *Crunch!*, was recorded in 10 days and released in April, 1990. Despite failing to make the charts, it would have done Madness proud in their heyday and it left The Madness trailing in its wake. Ironically, the best track, *Magic Carpet*, had been co-written by Suggs during the death-throes of The Madness and if released then, would surely have seen the band back in the big time.

The name The Nutty Boys conjured up images of Madness and the early days of *One Step Beyond* and *Night Boat To Cairo*, and when Lee and Chris put a band together it was something that was going to dog their every move. Promoters, in an attempt to fill venues, made great play of the Madness connection, even to the point of claiming that it really was Madness, but under a new name. In fact only one Madness song was included in the set, *Take It Or Leave It*. Lee, for the record, proved to be an excellent frontman (as anyone who had seen any Madness videos or gigs could have guessed) and a decent singer too.

With everyone doing their own thing, it looked like Madness as a band were dead and buried. And then along came Virgin to put the cat amongst the pigeons with the 22 track greatest hits album and video package, *Divine Madness*. It was released in February, 1992, with a massive promotional push including TV advertising, and it was destined for only one spot. Numero uno in the album and video charts. At the same time, *It Must Be Love*, was released as a single and Madness were back in the Top Ten singles chart too. The funny thing was, the very same single had been released in

"We did this gig in Colchester and the management had the bright idea of putting MADNESS AS THE NUTTY BOYS LIVE! outside the gig in big pink letters. How we laughed! I told them to take it down and the gig was alright, but this girl kept shouting, 'You've sold out!', and I thought, 'Funny, the place looks half-empty'."

Chrissy Boy

Below: The Nutty Boys with Chris (far right) and Lee (right foreground) (Nil Satis/Gavin Watson)

(Virgin)

"If we do reform, it will have to be really really good. I wouldn't do it any other way. I'd even record some stuff and if it was bad, I wouldn't put it out. I think that's how everyone feels."

Bedders

May, 1989, when the song was used as the theme tune to the film, *The Tall Guy*, which saw Suggs appear in a cameo role, but it did nothing.

Even before the release of *Divine Madness*, there was rumours that the band were about to reform. Articles appeared in the tabloids and the music press saying that the band were all set to make a comeback, and the more it was said the more it looked like happening. Barso was now back in North London and had been writing with Suggs, but only Chas was publicly saying that he hoped the band would reform.

A gig at the Dublin Castle which was advertised with the teaser "Is this the return of the Los Palmas 7?" built up a lot of people's hopes that a secret Madness gig was in the offing, but despite the appearance of Chris, Lee and Bedders on stage, this was no Madness reunion. Instead it was the Terry Edwards Allstars strutting their stuff with the help of a few friends, and the only Madness tune all night was *Benny Bullfrog*.

89

Then, at the start of April, and just when it looked like the rumours would come to nothing, Madness turned up at Notre Dame Hall in London's Leicester Square, and played for the first time as a seven piece since December 21st, 1983. They ran through four songs, *It Must Be Love*, *House Of Fun* (twice) and *Madness* for the benefit of an invited audience and a film crew from Go TV!. The secret gig was to be part of a pilot show for a new late night music programme on Channel 4, and Chas had persuaded the others to do the gig at the very last minute.

The Madness train was once again getting ready to roll and the offers of gigs started to pour in. Chas was buzzing by this time and continually trying to get the others to reform, but at various times at least one or two of the band didn't want to do it. A lot of the songs had been written to capture certain times and the feeling was that those times had past and the band had moved on. At the end of the day though, nobody was living in the lap of luxury - Lee had even been working on the bins to make a living - and it was the promise of big money that was going to get them back on the stage.

The Mean Fiddler wanted to stage an open-air concert in Finsbury Park, but despite the prospect of a big pay day on their own doorstep, not everyone wanted to do it. Chris seemed the least interested, but when he was finally talked into it by Suggs and Barso, Suggs then decided that he didn't really want to get the band back together. And so it went on until all of the band agreed in unison to do the gig and the magnificent 7 were all set to ride again.

Saturday, August the 8th was the big day for what was to be called Madstock. 36,000 people were invited to the Madness reunion and farewell gig the band never had at £20 a head (ouch). A year before, and few would have believed that so many people would turn up to see the band, but such was the demand for tickets that a repeat performance was arranged for the following day and a further 36,000 bodies were set to descend on Finsbury Park.

Also on the bill were Ian Dury & The Blockheads, Morrissey and Camden bands, Flowered Up and Gallon Drunk, but there was no mistaking who the vast majority of people had come to see. Morrissey didn't even turn up for the second day following the poor reception he received on the Saturday.

For their part, Madness had been preparing for the gig with a week's rehearsals in London followed by another week's worth in Holland where they also played a warm-up gig in a small club in The Hague.

When they walked on to the stage at Finsbury Park that Saturday evening any remaining cobwebs were blown away by the reception they received, and it was just like old times again. The boys ran through all the favourites, with the entire audience singing along to every song, and it was hard to say who was enjoying themselves the most, the band or the fans. Such was the power of the noise generated that a minor earthquake was recorded - just as *The Prince* had promised all those years before - and nearby tower blocks joined the party by swaying to the beat. And speaking of royalty, none other than Prince Buster himself joined Madness on stage to round off the perfect evening's entertainment.

"The band will reform at 9.30pm and turn back into pumpkins an hour and a half later."
Madstock press release

Right: Suggs
(Streetlink / Martin Dean)

The whole show was recorded and a video and album, entitled *Madstock!*, came out on Go! Discs that October. The Madness comeback was complete when a new single, a cover of Jimmy Cliff's *The Harder They Come*, was released and Madness appeared on *Top Of The Pops* via a satellite link that saw the band performing live in Moscow's Red Square of all places. The only one not present was Lee, who was refused entry to Russia because of his criminal record picked up when he was but a kid.

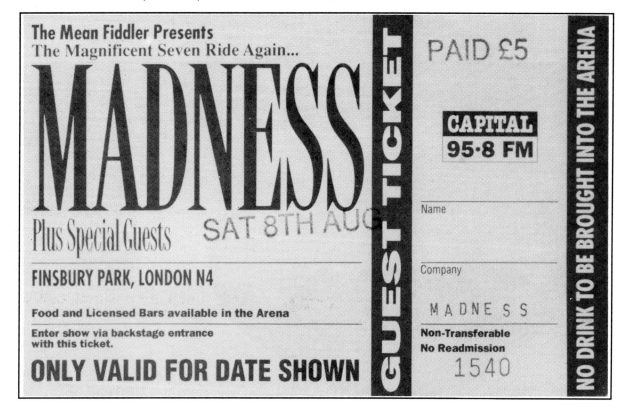

It didn't stop there either. A seven date tour of Britain, taking in the biggest venues in the largest cities, saw Madness back on the road just before Christmas. The tour kicked off with two nights at Wembley Arena and finished at Birmingham NEC on December 22nd. Again, the venues were packed to see Madness, with support bands The Farm, who Suggs now managed and had produced a number one album for, and 808 State, simply making up the numbers.

That Christmas also saw Madness on British TV, with Channel 4 showing an hour-long version of Madstock, and the band doing a commercial for Sekonda watches. To the tune of *Madness*, the band did a little ditty about Sekonda and did the nutty train dance around a jeweller's shop. Beware of expensive imitations ran the slogan which proved just as apt for the band, given the fact that the current craze for cover bands had spawned both Utter Madness in the U.K. and Mad Not Madness in Australia.

And so to 1993. Already Madness have appeared at a number of major gigs on the Continent and there is also talk of another round of U.K. dates this coming Christmas. It is still a very fluid situation with few concrete plans, and it hasn't stopped the boys getting on with other things, but at least a whole new crop of fans has been given the opportunity to see one of the truly great bands England has produced in recent years.

What ever the future brings, fans of Madness will always have memories to keep and records to play. Chrissy Boy once said that he wanted people to talk about the Madness sound in years to come. That'll happen no problem.

In years to come, Madness will be remembered as one of pop's success stories of the 1980s, but to fans of the band they will always be so much more than a pile of hit singles and a collection of great albums. To those brought up on the mad monster sound, Madness were everything at a time when bands enjoyed followings as passionate as any football team's. Sure it's great to catch an old Madness tune on the radio now and again, and everyone and their dog will tell you that they liked Madness. But where it was really at was being slap bang in the middle of a packed hall, with sweat dripping off the walls and enough atmosphere to make the moon inhabitable, and the chants of "Madness!" getting louder and louder until there they were, on the stage in front of you. Madness. Seven ordinary blokes from North London who captured the hearts and minds of kids the world over.

Two words. "Hey you!". That's all it took for Chas Smash to have the entire audience under the magical spell that was Madness. And in fifty years time, those same two words will still be filling dancefloors, even if it is only at grab a granny nights down the local old folks' home.

Madness. They came, we saw, we had the time of our lives.

DISCOGRAPHY

(Stiff / Clare Muller)

MADNESS
The Singles

☐ **THE PRINCE / MADNESS**
2 Tone CHS TT3
Released: August 1979
Chart Best: No. 16
Reissued on Old Gold (OG 9685) in
February 1987

☐ **ONE STEP BEYOND / MISTAKES**
Stiff BUY 56
Released: October 1979
Chart Best: No. 7
Also available as 12" (Stiff BUYIT 56) with
additional track, **NUTTY THEME**.

☐ **MY GIRL / STEPPING INTO LINE**
Stiff BUY 62
Released: December 1979
Chart Best: No. 3

Also available on 12" (Stiff BUYIT 62) with
additional track, **IN THE RAIN**.
7" reissued by Virgin (VS 781) in June 1985,
and **MY GIRL** reissued again by Virgin in
July 1992 with **MADNESS (Live)** (VS 1425).
This time it was also available on two
different CD singles, one featuring **MY
GIRL, E.R.N.I.E. (Live),
EMBARRASSMENT (Live)**, and
TOMORROW'S DREAMS (Live) (VSCDG
1425) and one featuring **MY GIRL,
PRECIOUS ONE (Live), MY GIRL (Live)**
and **DISAPPEAR (Live)** (VSCDT 1425).

☐ **WORK, REST AND PLAY EP** featuring
**NIGHT BOAT TO CAIRO / DECEIVES THE
EYE / THE YOUNG AND THE OLD / DON'T
QUOTE ME ON THAT**

(Stiff)

Madness

our house

new single
STIFF RECORDS buy 163

Stiff BUY 71
Released: March 1980
Chart Best: No. 6
Reissued by Virgin (VS782) in June 1985.

☐BAGGY TROUSERS / THE BUSINESS
Stiff BUY 84
Released: September 1980
Chart best: No. 3
BAGGY TROUSERS was reissued on Old
Gold (OG 9821) with EMBARRASSMENT in
November, 1988.

☐EMBARRASSMENT / CRYING SHAME
Stiff BUY 102
Released: November 1980
Chart best: No. 4

☐THE RETURN OF THE LOS PALMAS 7 /
THAT'S THE WAY TO DO IT
Stiff BUY 108
Released: January 1981
Chart best: No. 7
The 7" to this single came in two sleeves.
One has cartoon drawings of the band's
faces and Madness are billed as The Nutty
Boys. The other sleeve is a more standard
picture sleeve featuring the boys in a
canteen kitchen. Also available in both
sleeves as a 12" (Stiff BUYIT 108) with two
additional tracks, MY GIRL (as performed by
The Prince AKA Barso) and SWAN LAKE
(live).

☐SIX PACK
Stiff GRAB 1
Released: February 1981
This offering saw the first six Madness
singles collected together in a foldout plastic
presentation wallet and sold as a set.

☐GREY DAY / MEMORIES
Stiff BUY 112
Released: April 1981
Chart Best: No. 4
Also available on 12" (Stiff BUYIT 112) with
additional track, UN PASO ADELANTE, and
as a cassingle (ZBUY 112) with no
additional tracks.
7" reissued by Virgin (VS783) in June 1985.

☐SHUT UP / A TOWN WITH NO NAME
Stiff BUY 126
Released: September 1981
Chart Best: No. 7
Also available on 12" (Stiff BUYIT 126) with
additional track, NEVER ASK TWICE.

☐IT MUST BE LOVE / SHADOW ON THE
HOUSE
Stiff BUY 134
Released: November 1981
Chart Best: No. 4
Also available on 12" (Stiff BUYIT 134) with
no additional tracks.
IT MUST BE LOVE reissued by Old Gold
(OG 9826) with MY GIRL in November,
1988, then by Virgin (VS 1197) with
RETURN OF THE LOS PALMAS 7 in May
1989 when it was used as the theme tune to
the film, The Tall Guy, and again by Virgin in
February 1992 to coincide with the release
of the DIVINE MADNESS LP. This time, IT
MUST BE LOVE was back in the top ten
backed by BED AND BREAKFAST MAN
(VS1405) and available as a CD single
(VSCDT 1405) with the additional tracks
AIRPLANE and DON'T QUOTE ME ON
THAT.

☐CARDIAC ARREST / IN THE CITY
Stiff BUY 140
Released: February 1982
Chart Best: No. 14
Also available on 12" (Stiff BUYIT 140) with
no additional tracks, but CARDIAC ARREST
is an extended version.

☐HOUSE OF FUN / DON'T LOOK BACK
Stiff BUY 146
Released: May 1982
Chart Best: No. 1
Also available on 12" (Stiff BUYIT 146) and
as 7" picture disc (Stiff P-BUY 146) with no
additional tracks.
7" reissued by Virgin (VS784) in June 1985,
and HOUSE OF FUN reissued again by
Virgin with UN PASO ADELANTE (VS1413)
in April 1992. This time around it was
available in 12" (VST 1413) and CD single
(VSCDT 1413) with the additional tracks,
YESTERDAY'S MEN and GABRIEL'S
HORN.

Above: Chrissy Boy performing under water for the *It Must Be Love* video. He had to fill his pockets with lead weights to stop him floating to the surface and nearly drowned himself in the process (Stiff).

☐DRIVING IN MY CAR / ANIMAL FARM
Stiff BUY 153
Released: July 1982
Chart Best: No. 4
Also available in 7" poster sleeve and as a 7" picture disc (Stiff P-BUY 153) with no additional tracks, and on 12" (Stiff SBUY 153) with the additional track, **RIDING ON MY BIKE**.
7" reissued by Virgin (VS785) in June 1985.

☐OUR HOUSE / WALKING WITH MR. WHEEZE
Stiff BUY 163
Released: November 1982
Chart Best: No. 5
Also available as 7" with **OUR HOUSE (Special Stretch Mix)** (Stiff BUYJB 163), 7" picture disc (Stiff P-BUY 163) with no additional tracks and on 12" (Stiff BUYIT 163) which features **OUR HOUSE (extended)**, the standard 7" version of **OUR HOUSE** (although not listed) and **WALKING WITH MR. WHEEZE**.

7" reissued by Virgin (VS786) in June 1985.

☐TOMORROW'S (JUST ANOTHER DAY) / MADNESS (IS ALL IN THE MIND)
Stiff BUY 169
Released: February 1983
Chart Best: No. 8
Also available as a 7" picture disc (Stiff P-BUY 169) with no additional tracks and on 12" with **TOMORROW'S (JUST ANOTHER DAY) (Warped 12" Version)**, a re-recorded version of the same song with Elvis Costello on vocals and an additional track, **BLUE BEAST (Warp Mix)**.
7" (VS787) and 12" (VS787/12) reissued by Virgin in June 1985.

☐WINGS OF A DOVE / BEHIND THE 8 BALL
Stiff BUY 181
Released: August 1983
Chart Best: No. 2
Also available in two different picture sleeves, as 7" picture disc (Stiff P-BUY 181)

101

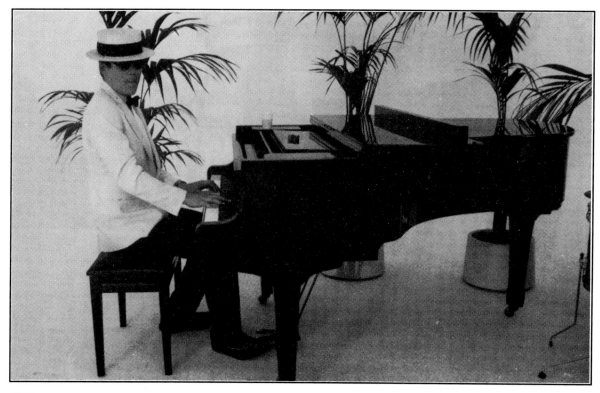

(Stiff)

with no additional tracks and on 12" with the additional track, **ONE'S SECOND THOUGHTLESSNESS**.
7" (VS788) and 12" (VS 788/12) reissued by Virgin in June 1985.

☐THE SUN AND THE RAIN / FIREBALL XL5
Stiff BUY 192
Released: October 1983
Chart Best: No. 5
Also available on 7" picture disc (Stiff P-BUY 192) with no additional tracks and on 12" with an extended version of **THE SUN AND THE RAIN** and the additional track, **MY GIRL (Live)**.
7" (VS789) and 12" (VS789/12) reissued by Virgin in June 1985.

☐MICHAEL CAINE / IF YOU THINK THERE'S SOMETHING
Stiff BUY 196
Released: January 1984
Chart Best: No. 11
Also available on 7" picture disc (Stiff P-BUY 196) with no additional tracks and on 12" (Stiff BUYIT 196) with no additional tracks, although **MICHAEL CAINE** appears

as an extended version as well as the standard one.
7" (VS790) and 12" (VS790/12) reissued by Virgin in June 1985.

☐ONE BETTER DAY / GUNS
Stiff BUY 201
Released: May 1984
Chart Best: No. 17
Also available as 7" with poster sleeve and 7" picture disc (Stiff P-BUY 201) with no additional tracks and on 12" (Stiff BUYIT 201) with the additional tracks, **VICTORIA GARDENS (Remix)** and **SARAH**.

☐YESTERDAY'S MEN / ALL I KNEW
Zarjazz JAZZ 5
Released: August 1985
Chart Best: No. 18
Also available as a two single pack (Zarjazz JAZZSD 5) with one being a square picture disc and the other a standard 7" with additional tracks, **YESTERDAY'S MEN (Harmonica £6 Mix)** and **IT MUST BE LOVE (Live)**, and on 12" (Zarjazz JAZZ 5-12) with no additional tracks but with **YESTERDAY'S MEN** appearing in both an extended and a demo version.

UNCLE SAM / PLEASE DON'T GO
Zarjazz JAZZ 7
Released: October 1985
Chart Best: No. 21
Also available as a 7" in a plastic Flag Bag with the stars and stripes (Zarjazz JAZZSD 7), as a 7" picture disc (Zarjazz JAZZY 7) with the additional track, **INANITY OVER CHRISTMAS**, and on 12" (Zarjazz JAZZ 7-12) with no additional tracks but with **UNCLE SAM** appearing in both a Raygun Mix and an eight track demo version.

SWEETEST GIRL / JENNIE (A PORTRAIT OF)
Zarjazz JAZZ 8
Released: January 1986
Chart Best: No. 35
Also available as a 7" one-sided picture disc (Zarjazz JAZZY 8) with no additional tracks, as a 7" Valentine's Day double pack with the extra single featuring **TEARS YOU CAN'T HIDE** and **CALL ME**, and on 12" with no additional tracks but with **SWEETEST GIRL** appearing in both a dub and an extended version.

sleeve and with an 8 page colour souvenir booklet on Madness adapted from Dave Hill's book, *Designer Boys And Material Girls: Manufacturing The '80s Pop Dream* (Blandford Press).

PEEL SESSIONS featuring THE PRINCE, BED AND BREAKFAST MAN, LAND OF HOPE AND GLORY and STEPPING INTO LINE
Strange Fruit SFPS 007
Released: October 1986
The above is a 12" release, but was also available as a cassingle (Strange Fruit SFPSC 007) and as a CD single (Strange Fruit SFPSCD 007) with no additional tracks.

THE HARDER THEY COME / TOMORROW'S JUST ANOTHER DAY / TAKE IT OR LEAVE IT
Go! Discs GOD93
Released: October 1992

Chart Best: No. 44
Also available as a cassingle (GODMC93) with no additional tracks, and a CD (GODCD93) with the additional track, **TAKE IT OR LEAVE IT**. All of the tracks are live and from the Madstock gig in August, 1992.

NIGHT BOAT TO CAIRO / NIGHT BOAT TO CAIRO (Paul Gotel Rude Edit)
Virgin VS1447
Released: March 1993
Also available as a cassingle (VSC1447) with no additional tracks and as a 12" (VSCT1447) and CD (VSCDT 1447) both with three extra mixes, **Paul Gotel Rude**

(WAITING FOR) THE GHOST TRAIN / MAYBE IN ANOTHER LIFE
Zarjazz JAZZ 9
Released: October 1986
Chart Best: No. 18
Also available on a shaped picture disc (Zarjazz JAZZS 9) with no additional tracks, on 12" (Zarjazz JAZZ9-12) with the additional track **SEVEN YEAR SCRATCH** which is a medley of Madness hits by DJ Noel Watson, and as a limited edition 12" with the same tracks, but in a gatefold

The Sun and the Rain

by Madness

now a picture disc

7" buy 192 12" buy it 192
picture disc p buy 192

Mix, Well Hung Parliament Dub Edit and **Paul Gotel Rude Instrumental**. Only the first track is by Madness. The others are studio mixes that bare little resemblance to the old Madness favourite and are aimed squarely at today's dance / rave scene.

At the time of writing, Virgin were planning to release all the Madness singles, both A and B sides, in a CD box set with booklet.

MADNESS
The Albums

☐ONE STEP BEYOND
Stiff SEEZ 17
Released: October 1979
Chart Best: No. 2
Side One: **One Step Beyond / My Girl / Night Boat To Cairo / Believe Me / Land Of Hope & Glory / The Prince / Tarzan's Nuts**
Side Two: **In The Middle Of The Night / Bed And Breakfast / Razor Blade Alley / Swan Lake / Rockin' In Ab / Mummy's Boy / Madness / Chipmunks Are Go**
Also available in cassette format (Stiff ZSEEZ 17)
Reissued by Virgin on vinyl (OVED 133), cassette (OVEDC 133) and on CD (OVEDCD 133).

☐ABSOLUTELY
Stiff SEEZ 29
Released: September 1980
Chart Best: No. 2
Side One: **Baggy Trousers / Embarrassment / E.R.N.I.E. / Close Escape / Not Home Today / On The Beat Pete / Solid Gone**
Side Two: **Take It Or Leave It / Shadow Of Fear / Disappear / Overdone / In The Rain / You Said / Return Of The Los Palmas 7**
This album came in two slightly different sleeves, each featuring a different photo from the same session, and also in cassette format (ZSEEZ 29).

Reissued by Virgin on vinyl (OVED 134), cassette (OVDC 134) and on CD (OVCD 134) in August 1988.

☐ 7
Stiff SEEZ 39
Released: October 1981
Chart Best: No. 5
Side One: **Cardiac Arrest / Shut Up / Sign Of The Times / Missing You / Mrs. Hutchison / Tomorrow's Dream**
Side Two: **Grey Day / Pac-A-Mac / Promises Promises / Benny Bullfrog / When Dawn Arrives / The Opium Eaters / Day On The Town**
Also available in cassette format (Stiff ZSEEZ 39)
Reissued by Virgin on vinyl (OVED 135), cassette (OVMC 135) and on CD (OVCD 135) in August 1988.

☐COMPLETE MADNESS
Stiff HIT-TV 1
Released: April 1992
Chart Best: No. 1
Side One: **Embarrassment / Shut Up / My Girl / Baggy Trousers / It Must Be Love / The Prince / Bed And Breakfast Man / Night Boat To Cairo**
Side Two: **House Of Fun / One Step Beyond / Cardiac Arrest / Grey Day / Take It Or Leave It / In The City / Madness / Return Of The Los Palmas 7**
Also available in cassette format (Stiff ZHIT-TV 1).

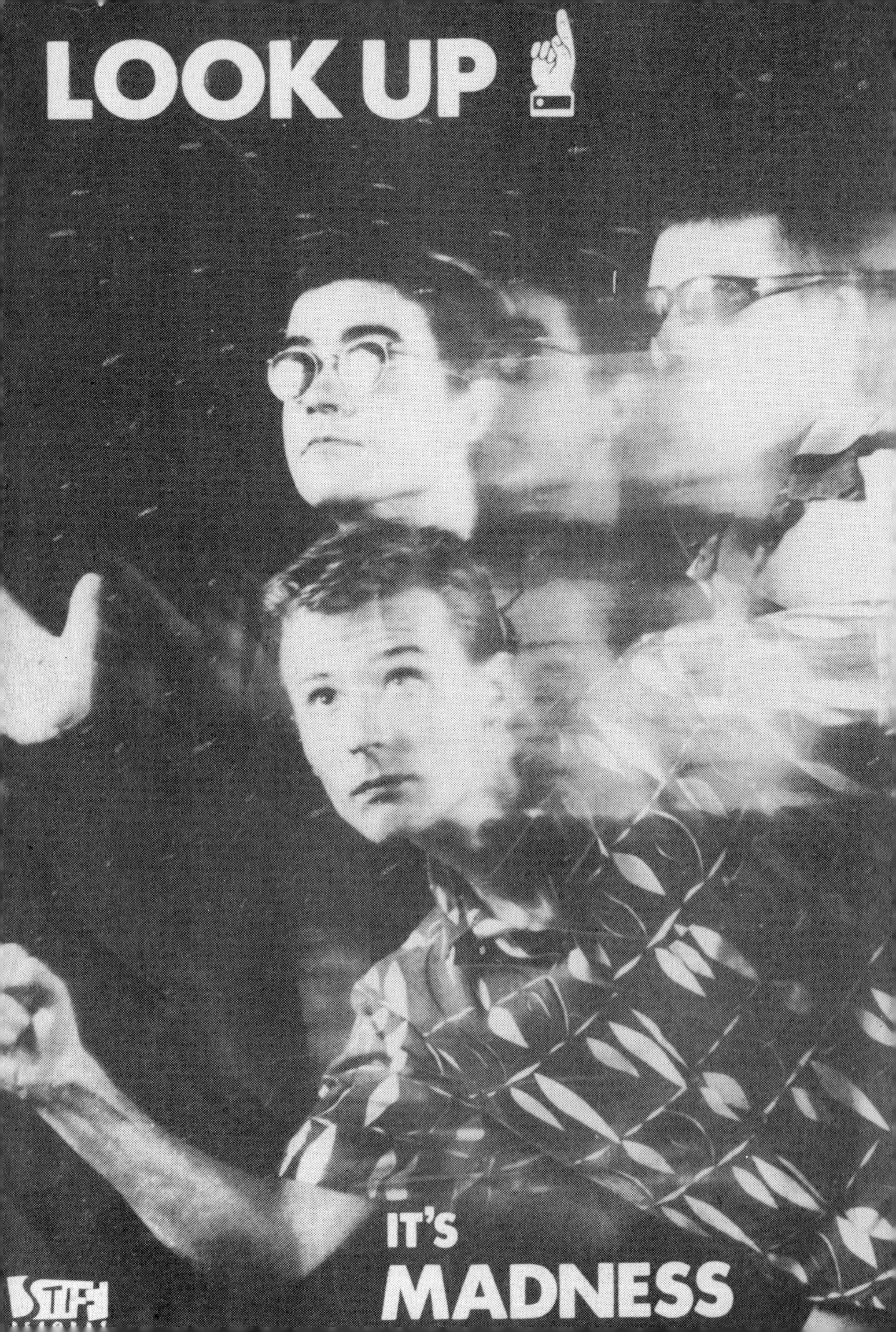
LOOK UP
IT'S
MADNESS

NEW SINGLE

Wings of a Dove
c/w Behind the 8 Ball

Reissued on CD by Virgin (HITCD 1) in July 1988.

THE RISE AND FALL
Stiff SEEZ 46
Released: October 1982
Chart Best: No. 10
Side One: **Rise And Fall / Tomorrow's (Just Another Day) / Blue Skinned Beast / Primrose Hill / Mr. Speaker (Gets The Word) / Sunday Morning**
Side Two: **Our House / Tiptoes / New Delhi / That Face / Calling Cards / Are You Coming (With Me) / Madness (Is All In The Mind)**
Also available in cassette format (Stiff ZSEEZ 46)
Reissued by Virgin on vinyl (OVED 191), cassette (OVMC 191) and CD (OVCD 191) in August 1988.

KEEP MOVING
Stiff SEEZ 53
Released: February 1984
Chart Best: No. 6
Side One: **Keep Moving / Wings Of A Dove / Turning Blue / One Better Day / March Of The Gherkins / Michael Caine**
Side Two: **Prospects / Victoria Gardens / Samantha / One Better Day / Give Me A Reason / Turning Blue**
Also available in cassette format (Stiff ZSEEZ 53) and picture disc (Stiff PSEEZ53)
Reissued by Virgin on vinyl (OVED 191), cassette (OVMC 191) and CD (OVCD 191) in August 1988.

MAD NOT MAD
Zarjazz JZLP-1
Released: September 1985
Chart Best: No. 16
Side One: **I'll Compete / Yesterday's Men / Uncle Sam / White Heat / Mad Not Mad**
Side Two: **Sweetest Girl / Burning The Boats / Tears You Can't Hide / Time / The Coldest Day**
Also available on cassette (Zarjazz JZMC-1) and one-sided CD (Zarjazz JZCD-1).

UTTER MADNESS
Zarjazz JZLP-2
Released: November 1986
Chart Best: No. 29
Side One: **Our House / Driving In My Car / Michael Caine / Wings Of A Dove / Yesterday's Men / Tomorrow's Just Another Day / I'll Compete**
Side Two: **(Waiting For) The Ghost Train / Uncle Sam / The Sun And The Rain / Sweetest Girl / One Better Day / Victoria Gardens**
Also available on cassette (Zarjazz JZMC-2) with no additional tracks and on CD (Zarjazz JZCD-2) with the additional track, **Seven Year Scratch (Hits Megamix)**.

IT'S MADNESS
Pickwick VVIP 107
Released: September 1990
Side One: **House Of Fun / Don't Look Back / Wings Of A Dove / The Young And The Old / My Girl / Stepping Into Line / Baggy Trousers / The Business**
Side Two: **Embarrassment / One's Second Thoughtlessness / Grey Day / Memories / It Must Be Love / Deceives The Eye / Driving In My Car / Animal Farm**
Also available on CD (VVIPD 107) with no additional tracks.

IT'S MADNESS . . . TOO
Pickwick VVIPD 115 (CD only)
Released: October 1991
Tracks: **The Prince / Madness / One Step Beyond / Mistakes / Return Of The Los Palmas 7 / Night Boat To Cairo / Shut Up / Town With No Name / Cardiac Arrest / In The City / Our House / Walking With Mr. Wheeze / Tomorrow's (Just Another Day) / Victoria Gardens / The Sun And The Rain / Michael Caine**
The first Pickwick release sold very well, but because sales of Pickwick collections tend to be through petrol stations, supermarkets and so on, it never appeared in the charts. The second release looked like doing even better, but it was withdrawn when their success spurred Virgin on to release DIVINE MADNESS.

☐DIVINE MADNESS
Virgin V 2692 (double album)
Released: February 1992
Chart Best: No. 1
Side One: **The Prince / One Step Beyond / Bed And Breakfast Man / My Girl / Night Boat To Cairo / Baggy Trousers**
Side Two: **Embarrassment / The Return Of The Los Palmas 7 / Grey Day / Shut Up / It Must Be Love**
Side Three: **Cardiac Arrest / House Of Fun / Driving In My Car / Our House / Tomorrow's Just Another Day / Wings Of A Dove**
Side Four: **The Sun And The Rain / Michael Caine / One Better Day / Yesterday's Men / Uncle Sam / The Sweetest Girl / (Waiting For) The Ghost Train**
Also available on cassette (MCV 2692) and on CD (CDV 2692), but without **Bed And Breakfast Man** and **The Sweetest Girl**.
It was the success of this album that brought a renewed flood of offers more Madness to reform and finally saw them come out of retirement.

☐MADSTOCK!
Go! Discs 828 367 - 1
Released: October 1992
Chart Best: No. 22
Side One: **One Step Beyond / The Prince / Embarrassment / My Girl / The Sun And The Rain / Grey Day / It Must Be Love / Shut Up / Driving In My Car**
Side Two: **Bed And Breakfast Man / Close Escape / Wings Of A Dove / Our House / Night Boat To Cairo / Madness / House Of Fun / Baggy Trousers / The Harder They Come**
Also available on cassette (828 367 - 3) and CD (828 367 - 4) with no additional tracks.

(Stiff)

MADNESS·One Better Day

109

MADNESS
The Videos

☐ **COMPLETE MADNESS**
Stiff HIT TV (Video) 1
Released: May 1982
Tracks: **The Prince / One Step Beyond /
Bed And Breakfast Man / My Girl / Night
Boat To Cairo / Baggy Trousers /
Embarrassment / The Return Of The Los
Palmas 7 / Grey Day / Shut Up / It Must Be
Love / Cardiac Arrest / House Of Fun** plus
the Japanese TV commercials for Honda
Reissued by Virgin (VVD 112) in May 1985.

☐ **TAKE IT OR LEAVE IT**
Virgin VVD 114
Released: May 1985
The Madness film that was made in 1981
and given only limited cinema release.
Highly recommended.

☐ **UTTER MADNESS**
Virgin VVD 180
Released: November 1986
Tracks: **Driving In My Car / Our House /
Tomorrow's Just Another Day / Wings Of
A Dove / The Sun And The Rain / Michael
Caine / One Better Day / Yesterday's Men
/ Uncle Sam / The Sweetest Girl / (Waiting
For) The Ghost Train**

☐ **DIVINE MADNESS**
Virgin VVD 1003
Released: February 1992
Tracks: **The Prince / One Step Beyond /
Bed And Breakfast Man / My Girl / Night
Boat To Cairo / Baggy Trousers /
Embarrassment / The Return Of The Los
Palmas 7 / Grey Day / Shut Up / It Must Be
Love / Cardiac Arrest / House Of Fun /
Driving In My Car / Our House /
Tomorrow's Just Another Day / Wings Of
A Dove / The Sun And The Rain / Michael
Caine / One Better Day / Yesterday's Men
/ Uncle Sam / The Sweetest Girl / (Waiting
For) The Ghost Train / I Pronounce You***
plus Japanese TV commercials for Honda
***I Pronounce You** is by The Madness.

☐**MADSTOCK!**
Polygram 086 014-3
One Step Beyond / The Prince / Embarrassment / My Girl / The Sun And The Rain / Land Of Hope And Glory / Grey Day / Razor Blade Alley / It Must Be Love / Tomorrow's Just Another Day / Take It Or Leave It / Shut Up / Driving In My Car / Bed And Breakfast Man / Close Escape / Wings Of A Dove / Our House / Night Boat To Cairo / Madness / Swan Lake / House Of Fun / Rockin' In Ab / Baggy Trousers / The Harder They Come

As you'll see from the above track listings, **DIVINE MADNESS** has more or less made **COMPLETE MADNESS** and **UTTER MADNESS** redundant. That said, at the time of writing you can buy **COMPLETE MADNESS** and **UTTER MADNESS** for the price of **DIVINE MADNESS** (that goes for the albums too). **MADSTOCK!** the video offers the best record of the Finsbury Park festival because not only do you get to see the band in action, you also get extra tracks too.

Madness have appeared on various compilation albums that won't be listed here, but two compilation videos are worth tracking down. **DANCE CRAZE** (Chrysalis CVHS 5022) features six live Madness tracks (**THE PRINCE, SWAN LAKE, RAZOR BLADE ALLEY, MADNESS, NIGHT BOAT TO CAIRO AND ONE STEP BEYOND**) from 1980, while **PUNK AND ITS AFTERSHOCKS** (STUD!O K7 010) captures three tracks (**THE PRINCE, SWAN LAKE and MY GIRL**) and an interview with the band in a pub from late '79. Young pups they look too.

MADNESS
The Flexis

☐**A FEW MINUTES OF MADNESS**
Lyntone 8680
Released: April 1981
Free with *Patches* Magazine

☐**TAKE IT OR LEAVE IT**
Lyntone 10353
Released: October 1981
Square flexi free with *Event* Magazine

☐**CAROLE ON 45**
Lyntone 10719
Released: December 1981
Free to members of M.I.S. with *Nutty Boys* Comic No. 4

☐**MY GIRL (Ballad)**
Lyntone 11546
Released: April 1982
Free with *Flexipop* Magazine

MADNESS
Other U.K. Releases

☐**DON'T QUOTE ME ON THAT / SWAN LAKE (Live)**
MAD 1
Released: March 1980
A 12" Hot Biscuit Promo of which only 500 were pressed.

☐**M.I.S. PLAYERS PRESENT**
M.I.S. cassette
Released: April 1982
Fan club only release.

☐**THE MAD NOT MAD PARTY**
JUMP SPELP1
Released: March 1986
Live promo LP on blue vinyl including old favourites and **MAD NOT MAD** tracks, but also **LISTEN TO YOUR FATHER** (with Feargal Sharkey on vocals) and two tracks from a *Whistle Test* appearance, **BURNING THE BOATS** and **TIME**.

☐**LIVE TRACKS 1979-86**
M.I.S. cassette
Released: 1987
Again, a fan club only release.

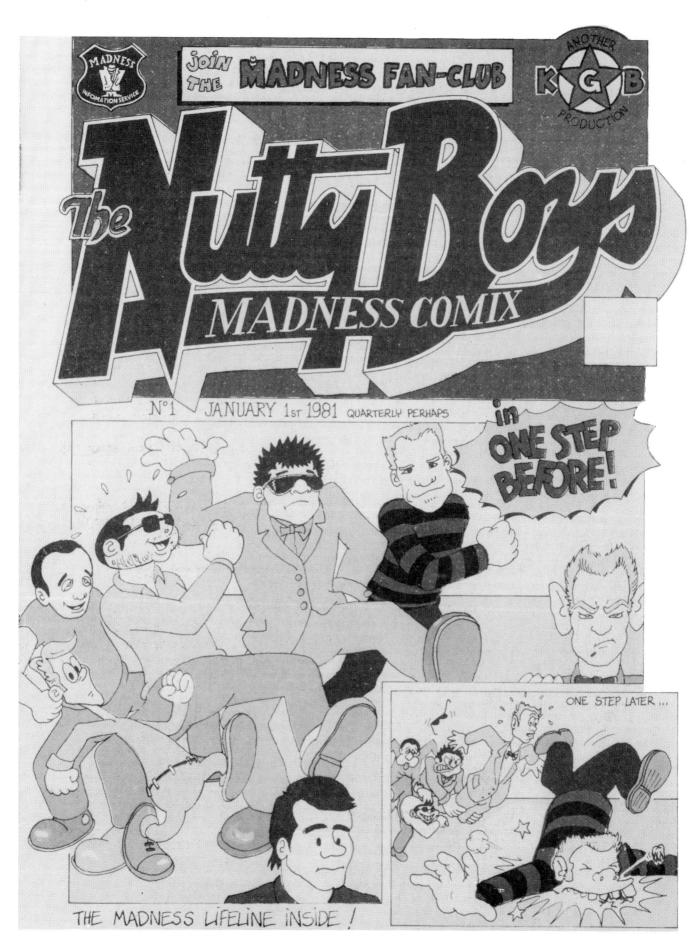

MADNESS
Foreign Releases

It would be pointless to list all foreign releases since most are no different from U.K. releases. They are still becoming increasingly collectable though, particularly when they appear in a different picture sleeve or a picture sleeve for the first time, as with foreign releases of **THE PRINCE**. Japanese releases are always worth picking up as they usually include lyric sheets and other inserts. Below are a few choice gems to squander your hard earned money on at the next record fair.

☐**TARZAN'S NUTS / NIGHT BOAT TO CAIRO**
7" single only released in Holland
☐**ONE STEP BEYOND / MISTAKES**
Limited number of Belgian pressing came in orange vinyl
☐**MY GIRL / STEPPING INTO LINE**
Limited number of Belgian pressing came in orange vinyl
☐**WORK REST & PLAY**
Available in Italy on 12" with **ONE STEP BEYOND** appearing in its Italian form, **UN PASO AVANTI.**
☐**NUTTY BOYS**
Another 12" from Italy with **GREY DAY, RETURN OF THE LOS PALMAS 7, MEMORIES** and **THAT'S THE WAY TO DO IT.**
☐**MADNESS AS NUTTY BOYS**
Japanese mini-LP with lyric sheet featuring six tracks, **RETURN OF THE LOS PALMAS 7, IN THE RAIN, SWAN LAKE (Live), MY GIRL, ONE STEP BEYOND** and **BAGGY TROUSERS.**
☐**GREY DAY**
Another six track mini-LP from Japan with lyric sheet featuring **GREY DAY, THE YOUNG AND THE OLD, THE BUSINESS, DON'T QUOTE ME ON THAT, DECEIVES THE EYE** and **THAT'S THE WAY TO DO IT.**
☐**DANCE CRAZY**

Six track mini-LP from Australia featuring **GREY DAY, ONE STEP BEYOND, BAGGY TROUSERS, MEMORIES, THAT'S THE WAY TO DO IT** and **SWAN LAKE (Live).**
☐**MADNESS**
When Geffen picked up Madness in the U.S. they released this album with **OUR HOUSE, TOMORROW'S (JUST ANOTHER DAY), IT MUST BE LOVE, PRIMROSE HILL, SHUT UP, HOUSE OF FUN, NIGHT BOAT TO CAIRO (Remix), RISE AND FALL, BLUE SKINNED BEAST, CARDIAC ARREST, GREY DAY** and **MADNESS (IS ALL IN THE MIND).**

MADNESS
Books and Comics

Books on Madness are surprisingly thin on the ground. Here's a few to look out for.

☐**A BRIEF CASE HISTORY OF MADNESS**
By Mark Williams
Proteus 1982
32 page book with a good selection of photos, but a criminal lack of text. Long since out of print.

☐**LIMITED EDITION MADNESS**
By Tanya Smart
Gamester 1982
Not really a book, but number two of *Limited Edition Magazine*. It's 32 pages long and contains loads of photos and the usual hack text. Now out of print.

☐Songbooks were available for all the albums (Warner Bros.), but it might be difficult finding them now. To the rescue comes **DIVINE MADNESS** (EMI Music Publishing / IMP, 1992) which at least includes the band's greatest hits.

☐There were 13 copies of *The Nutty Boys* comic published between 1981 and 1988. Probably.

THE MADNESS
The Singles

☐ **I PRONOUNCE YOU / PATIENCE**
Virgin VS 1054
Released: March 1988
Chart Best: No. 44
Also available on 12" (VST 1054), CD (VSCD 1054) and as 7" EP box set, all with the additional tracks, **4BF** and **11TH HOUR**. The box set also included an enamel badge and two postcards.

☐ **WHAT'S THAT / GOOD BOY**
Virgin VS 1078
Released: May 1988
Also available on 12" (VST 1078) with additional track, **FLASHINGS**, and on two interlocking picture discs, one with **WHAT'S THAT / GOOD BOY** (VSS 1078) and the other with **WHAT'S THAT / FLASHINGS** (VSJ 1078).

THE MADNESS
The Album

☐ **THE MADNESS**
Virgin V 2507
Released: April 1988
Chart Best: No. 65
Side One: **Nail Down The Days / What's That / I Pronounce You / Oh / In Wonder**
Side Two: **Song In Red / Nightmare Nightmare / Thunder & Lightning / Beat The Bride / Gabriel's Horn**
Also available on cassette (TCV 2507) with no extra tracks and on CD (CDV 2507) with four extra tracks, **11th Hour**, **Be Good Boy**, **Flashings** and **4 B.F.**.

THE NUTTY BOYS
(Lee and Chris)
The Single

☐ **IT'S O.K., I'M A POLICEMAN / FIGHT AMONGST YOURSELVES**
Nil Satis NIL 0037
Released: December 1992
Also available on 12" (NIL 00312) and cassette (NIL 003MC), both with the additional track **BIRTHDAY GIRL**, and on CD (NIL 003CD) with two additional tracks, **BIRTHDAY GIRL** and **SAVING FOR A RAINY DAY**.

THE NUTTY BOYS
The Album

☐ **CRUNCH!**
Streetlink STR LP 001
Released: April 1990
Side One: **Magic Carpet / Always Innocent / Daydreams / Complications / Pop My Top**
Side Two: **Whistle / Pipedreams / Feur Elise / People / You Got It**
Also available on cassette (STR MC 001) with no additional tracks and CD (STR CD 001) with two additional tracks, **JUST DREAMING** and **WHISTLING (Re-Mix)**. Reissued on CD only by Dojo (DOJO CD 101) in January 1993.

In true Nutty Boys fashion, the album **CRUNCH!** was the work of just Lee and Chris, but for the single **IT'S O.K., I'M A POLICEMAN** a band of seven had been gathered. Even stranger were the rumours that the album was actually called **THE**

NUTTY BOYS and Lee and Chris went under the name of Crunch!, but a mix-up at the record company changed the course of nutty history good and proper.

THE FINK BROTHERS
(Suggs and Carl)
The Single

☐ **MUTANTS IN MEGA-CITY ONE /
MUTANT BLUES**
Zarjazz JAZZ 2
Released: January 1985
Chart Best: No. 50
Also available as a square picture disc (JAZZS 2) with no additional tracks, and on 12" (some with poster) (JAZZ 2 -12) with no additional tracks, but **MUTANTS IN MEGA-CITY ONE** appears in a **Mutie Mix** version.

I would appreciate any corrections or additions to the above for any future editions of this book.

George Marshall, S.T. Publishing, P.O. Box 12, Dunoon, Argyll. PA23 7BQ. Scotland.

TOP TWENTY
MADNESS SINGLES
OF ALL TIME

The following chart was worked out with points being awarded to each single for highest chart position reached and number of weeks in the chart. The verdict of the Madness public is as follows . . .

1. BAGGY TROUSERS
2. House Of Fun
3. Wings Of A Dove
4. Embarrassment
5. It Must Be Love
6. Our House
7. My Girl
8. One Step Beyond
9. Grey Day
10. The Sun And The Rain
11. Driving In My Car
12. The Return Of The Los Palmas 7
13. Work Rest And Play
14. Shut Up
15. Tomorrow's (Just Another Day)
16. Michael Caine
17. Cardiac Arrest
18. The Prince
19. (Waiting For) The Ghost Train
20. One Better Day

And for what it's worth, the author's top five
1. The Prince
2. Yesterday's Men
3. My Girl
4. Wings Of A Dove
5. (Waiting For) The Ghost Train

Also Available From S.T. Publishing

The following books are available direct from the publisher. We send all books post free in the United Kingdom, but ask overseas readers to write first before ordering. All orders and enquiries should be sent to S.T. Publishing, P.O. Box 12, Dunoon, Argyll. PA23 7BQ. Scotland (cheques and postal orders should be made payable to S.T. Publishing).

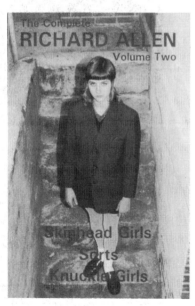

Richard Allen Is Back!

Back in the 1970s, Richard Allen was hailed as the king of youth cult fiction. He wrote 18 novels, with each one documenting the latest twist in youth cult fashion, from the million selling *Skinhead*, right through *Punk* and up to the mod revival and *Mod Rule*.

Then after *Mod Rule*, no more was heard from Allen. His books went out of print and the only place you could find them was by searching through second-hand bookshops and the like. More and more people started to collect them and as they became harder to find, the prices went up. Some dealers were charging £10 and more for paperbacks which originally cost as little as 30p!

Now all that has changed and the Richard Allen novels are once again available from S.T. Publishing. All 18 novels will be available, in six volumes of three. Currently available are *The Complete Richard Allen Volume One* and *The Complete Richard Allen Volume Two*, with *Volume Three* due out before the end of 1993.

The Complete Richard Allen Volume One follows the adventures of aggro merchant Joe Hawkins through three classic novels, *Skinhead*, *Suedehead* and *Skinhead Escapes*. Football matches, pub brawls, open-air pop concerts, hippies and Hell's Angels all give Joe and his skinhead gang chances to vent their sadistic violence. And even a prison sentence doesn't stop Joe Hawkins.

The Complete Richard Allen Volume Two is dedicated to the fairer sex, with *Skinhead Girls*, *Sorts* and *Knuckle Girls*. *Skinhead Girls* gives a girl's eye view of living for kicks, while *Sorts* follows the fortunes of a Smoothie girl who runs away and finds herself caught up in a world of sex, drugs - and murder. Finally, in Knuckle Girls you get to meet Glasgow's Ina Murray who fights for her rights - with a bicycle chain!

The Complete Richard Allen Volume Three will feature *Trouble For Skinhead*, *Skinhead Farewell* and *Top-Gear Skin*.

The Sunday Times Magazine described the Richard Allen novels as "low-life literature". We couldn't have put it better ourselves.

The Complete Richard Allen Volume One   U.K. Price £6.95
288 pages with full colour cover

The Complete Richard Allen Volume Two   U.K. Price £6.95
288 pages with full colour cover

S.T. Publishing - Putting The Boot Back Into Literature

Also Available From S.T. Publishing

SPIRIT OF '69 - A SKINHEAD BIBLE By George Marshall
168 A4 pages with countless photos
        For the first time, the history of the skinhead cult from the late Sixties to the present day. Tradition, music, aggro, style. It's all here and with no punches pulled. Nobody's claiming that skinheads are angels, but thanks to media sensationalism, the skinhead movement remains the most misunderstood youth cult of all time.   Now the skinheads tell their own story. There are chapters on the original skins, skinhead reggae, suedeheads and bootboys, Sham 69 and street punk, 2 Tone, Oi!, today's scene and skinhead fashion. Welcome to the land of the bovver brigade!   **U.K. Price £8.95**

THE TWO TONE STORY By George Marshall
110 A5 size pages with photos.
        1979. The dawning of a new era. The 2 Tone era. A time that was to see good old black and white dance music walk all over the colourful circus of pretty faces and false smiles that rock n' roll had become. This is the story of the rise and fall of 2 Tone, from the days when The Specials were called The Coventry Automatics, right through to the label's swansong with JB's Allstars. Relive the days when bands like The Beat, Madness, Bad Manners, The Selecter and The Bodysnatchers led the way on to the nation's dancefloors. Includes a full discography.   **U.K. Price £5.95**

WATCHING THE RICH KIDS By Arthur Kay
104 A5 pages with photos.
        We've all heard the one about the boy who picked up a guitar and found fame and fortune. Old chestnuts like that are ten a penny. But the stories that never get told are the ones about the kids who never get out of the starting blocks. Your genuine rags to rags tale. Meet Arthur Kay. A South London boy who has never lacked the talent, but who has never been given the opportunity to prove himself. From the hard mod bands of the Sixties to cult ska favourites, The Originals, and on to Oi! greats, The Last Resort, Arthur has always walked the back streets of rock n' roll. A world that has seen him go from reform school to crime to prison to drugs to drink. And still he managed to pick himself out of the gutter and gain a martial arts black belt. A street classic in every sense and one of the most important books we've published to date.   **U.K. Price £5.95**

If you would like to keep right up to date with the ska and other street scenes, send a large SSAE (U.K. only) or 2 IRCs (overseas and available from any post office) and we will send you the latest issue of Skinhead Times. It is a quarterly newspaper dedicated to the latest and greatest from the world of ska, reggae, Oi!, punk and the like. The address to write to is S.T. Publishing, P.O. Box 12, Dunoon, Argyll. PA23 7BQ. Scotland.

S.T. Publishing - Putting The Boot Back Into Literature

. . . Get arrested.

"We want people to talk about Madness for years to come."
Chrissy Boy, 1979.